THE POSSIBILITY OF SOMETHING HAPPENING

Graham Langmead

ATHENA PRESS
LONDON MIAMI

THE POSSIBILITY OF SOMETHING HAPPENING
Copyright © Graham Langmead 2002

ISBN 1 84401 002 3

First Published 2002 by
ATHENA PRESS LTD
Queen's House, 2 Holly Road
Twickenham, TW1 4EG
United Kingdom

Printed for Athena Press

THE POSSIBILITY OF
SOMETHING HAPPENING

Acknowledgements

My sincere thanks are due to my friends and colleagues and competitors whom I met in the London and North American insurance markets, especially those involved with Lloyd's, all of whom, individually and collectively, were part of my life in the insurance business. I am particularly grateful to David Larner for his interest and help during the preparation of this book, and to the following for their assistance along the way:

American Embassy, London
Frank Barber
Steven Berry
John Bird
Bloxham School, Oxfordshire
Malcolm Cannon
Palmer De Paulis
Phil Erickson
Alan Free
Vic Giles
David Jones
Theodore Landon
Wing Commander George Leatherbarrow
Lorraine Miller
Garry Redmond
Science Museum, Kensington
The telephone receptionists at the Statler Hilton and Waldorf Astoria Hotels, New York.

A very special thank you goes to my wife, Jean, whom I had the good fortune to meet in Chicago on one of my many visits to that city, where she was working as an executive secretary from England. Without her encouragement, patience, superb secretarial skills, and good humour, none of this would have got off the ground.

Graham Langmead, July 2001

About the Author

I was educated at Bloxham, passing school and higher school certificates and Oxford Responsions in 1940 when I was sixteen. I stayed on at Bloxham for two more years before joining the army, and spent that time working on the school farm, digging up the tennis courts to grow vegetables, taking the swill from the school kitchens to feed the pigs, and helping local farmers at harvest time for 4¾d (fourpence-three farthings – just under 2p in today's money) an hour. I was one of the buglers of the Officers' Training Corps, now known as the Cadet Force, who took turns each evening at nine o'clock to sound the last post at the school gate in memory of Old Bloxhamists who had lost their lives in the service of their country. Sadly, this ceremony has been discontinued. Out of a great-aunt's legacy I purchased a Morgan Super Sports three-wheeler for £10. A local farmer let me keep it in a barn close to the school. With the meagre wartime petrol ration, I and a chum or two would manage to get as far as Oxford for convivial evenings unbeknown, I presume, to the school staff who were a splendid bunch. They had even accepted salary cuts to help keep the school going when the number of pupils was down to less than ninety. I spent a lot of my time in the school library reading Shakespeare, Chaucer, historical books, novels such as *The Forsyte Saga*, and even *Mein Kampf* and *Das Kapital*.

In September 1942 I enlisted in the Grenadier Guards and was commissioned in the Oxfordshire and Buckinghamshire Light Infantry in May 1943. From then on I had a very interesting time, not without fear and excitement, in the Central Mediterranean Forces. I was personal prisoner's escort to General Von Vietinghoff when he surrendered the German forces in Italy. He informed me that as far as he was concerned it was only a temporary hiccup for the Germans. They and the French at the time of Dunkirk had agreed they would eventually run Europe between them, and this was the reason why France was permitted to have an unoccupied zone with its capital at Vichy. In December, 1945, at twenty-one, I was appointed as the Officer Commanding the British Company of the International Police Force – British/American/Russian/ French – which controlled the city of Vienna after World War II.

After that, what happened is set out in this book.

Uberrima Fides

An insurance contract is utterly dependent upon *Uberrima Fides* – 'Of the Utmost Good Faith'. This applies equally to the insurer and the insured. In common with every other commercial activity, insurance is not and never has been free of those who break this principle. The first recorded example occurred in the late 1500s when a merchant who had purchased a twelve months' Life Assurance policy died forty-nine weeks later. The insurers denied liability, declaring that the policy had already expired. They asserted that twelve months was the same as forty-eight weeks. Fortunately for the assured's dependants, Queen Elizabeth I ordered the insurers to honour the policy and pay. They did.

Contents

The Test

On a sunny afternoon in June during the 1970s, after a good lunch in the City, I went off to the West End to do a spot of shoplifting.

First call was the menswear department of Liberty's, where I took a fancy to a lightweight sports coat which I hid under my jacket. As I walked out of the department, red lights flashed on the short white pillars on each side of the exit. A very pleasant gentleman approached me.

'Excuse me, sir, but I think the assistant who sold you the garment you are carrying forgot to remove its security tag,' he said. 'If you try to remove this yourself, the garment will be damaged. Please accompany me back to the sales desk and we can put the matter to rights.'

My next call was at Miss Selfridge further down Regent Street. Just inside the front door were plastic baskets full of panties and bras of very little value. What on earth was I going to lift? At the rear of the shop I came across some beautiful diaphanous nightdresses. Stuffing one of these into my pocket, I left the shop and as I did so again noticed two red lights flashing. Once out into the sunlit street I wondered what would happen next. Before I had finished my musings I was conscious of an attractive young lady in step beside me who said, 'You've just nicked something from Miss Selfridge. I want you to come back to the shop with me.'

I burst out laughing, and she asked, 'This isn't *the test*, is it?'

I assured her that it was and that I would return to the shop with her without any more ado. On the way back, I asked what would have happened if I had refused. She left me in no doubt that her physical training as a store detective, including being a black belt judo expert, would have made it difficult for me to resist. As I had had advanced unarmed combat training in Special Forces, this could have developed into a splendid spectacle for passers-by in Regent Street!

These shoplifting adventures came about because the company within whose service I had worked my way from junior 'scratch boy' to senior broker and director, C. T. Bowring & Company – a multi-financial conglomerate having interests in insurance broking, insurance companies, hire purchase and merchant banking, with stores in Newfoundland, airport shops, a fleet of bulk cargo carriers, distribution of oils, and interests in various parts of Africa – had acquired a financial interest in a Florida company, Senelco, one of the pioneers in manufacturing security tags to be used mainly by clothing retailers as a major weapon against stealing. This method had only just been inaugurated, and insurance was required to protect the manufacturers and retailers using the tags against all manner of possible Third Party Liability claims, the most obvious being false arrest.

I found an underwriter at Lloyd's who was willing to issue such a policy, provided he could personally witness what would take place when an alleged shoplifter was apprehended through the use of the tags. The demonstrations were carefully set up so that senior personnel of the stores involved knew everything about the tests, including the actual day and times. The store detectives knew they would be taking place but were given no intimation of when.

Following the success of that afternoon's shenanigans, my underwriting friend was happy to suggest a premium for issuing a policy in respect of this further innovative insurance – just one example of Lloyd's underwriters and brokers working together with their clients to meet a new commercial need.

It is difficult to find a human activity in which insurance does not play a most important part.

For more than three hundred years Lloyd's of London have been innovators in the insurance business, having started in Edward Lloyd's Coffee House in the City of London.

The Coffee House

From the early 1500s the City of London developed into the major centre of commercial activities in England. There were, of course, others in outlying areas such as East Anglia and the city of Bristol, but the City of London became a bustling marketplace for all kinds of trading. From the mid-1500s to the late 1600s the population varied between 90,000 and 130,000 inhabitants, peaking just prior to the Plague of 1665 and reducing substantially following the Plague and the Great Fire in 1666. Paradoxically, the Great Fire played a major role in stamping out the horrors of the Plague.

There was very little, if any, commuting. In order to carry on their day-to-day business, the merchants lived within the City or just beyond its immediate edges. Many of the traders and their trades developed and thrived under the auspices of their respective Guilds and Livery Companies with their own headquarters or Halls, the most notable being the Mercers, Grocers, Drapers, Fishmongers, Goldsmiths, Skinners, Merchant Taylors, Haberdashers, Salters, Ironmongers, Vintners, and Clothworkers, known as the 'Great Twelve', whose order of seniority has been fixed since 1515. My own Livery Company, the Tallow Chandlers, is number twenty-one in order of seniority. There was intense rivalry between the Skinners and the Merchant Taylors which led to fierce disputes, even blows, as to which company was the sixth and which the seventh in order of precedence. This was sorted out by each being numbered both six and seven – hence the expression 'being at sixes and sevens'. Companies proliferated down the years until there are now over one hundred embracing all kinds of professions such as Chartered Accountants, Air Pilots and Air Navigators, Environmental Cleaners, Information Technologists, Scientific Instrument Makers, and so on. The Insurers, incorporated in 1979, is the ninety-second company.

However, there were many merchants who individually may

or may not have been members of such Guilds and Livery Companies. They used to meet with others of their kind in ale and gin houses as part of their day's work. As these places became disreputable, the merchants gravitated towards coffee houses which had sprung up in the early 1600s and had rapidly spread to all corners of London. In the public room of a coffee house would be tables ten to fifteen feet in length with high-backed benches on each side where the merchants would sit at their usual places, and all recognised each other's preferred seats. There would be other less formal tables and seats and a servery. Coffee houses were in effect clubs of a kind, with card playing, dice rolling, gossiping, news gathering and news spreading, and general business activities including buying and selling of merchandise, stocks and foreign currencies. Typical was Garraway's Coffee House close to the Royal Exchange.

In the mid-1680s, Edward Lloyd opened his first coffee house in Tower Street near the Church of All Hallows by the Tower, close to the neighbouring wharves on the River Thames in what is known as the Pool of London. The clientele which he attracted consisted not only of general merchants but also shipowners, sea captains, and others connected with overseas trade, and it was at Edward Lloyd's Coffee House where the foundations of the City of London's Marine insurance business originated and flourished.

This worked very simply. A merchant would let it be known amongst his friends and associates that he would be shipping a cargo to, say, North America, India, or the Far East, and he would enquire whether any others present would support him financially – to 'underwrite his venture'. A typical way would be for the merchant shipping the cargo to offer a comparatively small sum of money to other merchants, who would then pay him for the whole value of the cargo should it never arrive at its destination. Of course, if one was only talking about a single transaction, then the whole idea would be a non-starter. But if one was talking about many transactions, comparatively few of the thousands of cargoes being shipped would be lost and an overall profit could reasonably well be anticipated by those offering on a regular basis to underwrite the numerous and varied commercial ventures. In the same way, a shipowner would persuade other shipowners or merchants to do the same thing on behalf of the ship itself and his 'insurable interest' in it. Various merchants would each agree to accept a share of the risk involved in the venture on offer – for example, a particular cargo and/or a particular ship's voyage.

Insurable interest has remained a key factor for obtaining proper insurance of any kind. It is what differentiates *insurance* from straight *betting or wagering*. 'Insurable interest' is a very broad term but it has certain clear-cut limitations which can be demonstrated thus:

One may go into a betting shop and obtain odds that the monarch will be alive on a certain day, with no strings attached. That is a simple wager or bet, but in no way could it be regarded as an insurance policy, as there would be no demonstrable insurable interest. Such an attempt to *insure* the life of the monarch for no particular reason would not be acceptable. However, if one was involved in a project or activity which would have to be cancelled in the untimely event of the monarch dying or being taken seriously ill, there would quite clearly be a *contingent* insurable interest in the money already expended on that project.

There is one fundamental difference between life insurance, generally referred to as assurance, and all other forms of insurance: the former concerns the word *when* but the latter *all* concern the word *if*. The setting of rates in life assurance is dependent upon actuarial calculations derived from mortality tables produced by professional actuaries, and given the data available is an almost exact science. Obviously, there are statistics available for other forms of insurance, but they are still subject to the word *if*, and the greater the numbers of known units together with accidents or incidents, available for analysis, the more useful such statistics will be; with more unusual or sophisticated types of insurance, the greater the importance the human judgement factor will have to be. Just one comparison will suffice. There are many millions of motor cars having or not having accidents, compared with the number of communication satellites put or about to be put into orbit around the earth, successfully or otherwise, and every motor car and every communication satellite is a legitimate candidate for insurance.

In the beginning, deals were straightforward, man to man,

based on trust. It was as simple as, 'Mr Smith, sir, in consideration of your paying me £100 now, I will pay you £1,000 if and when we hear that your cargo or your ship has been lost.' Such considerations became known as premiums.

Later, instead of individual merchants or shipowners striking bargains among themselves, one man would undertake to arrange the deal on behalf of all those concerned in the venture. Hence syndicates of underwriters developed, and eventually it was not necessary for each member of such a syndicate to be personally present when the deal was struck. At this time the dictum of *Uberrima Fides* – Of the Utmost Good Faith – became paramount, and this was consistent with the adoption on the Lloyd's logo of the motto *Fidentia* – Self-confidence.

This was where the word 'underwriter' came to have two subtle differences of meaning. First, the individual risking his own money. Second, the individual who put not only his own money at risk but also the monies of others on behalf of whom he would also underwrite ventures – in short, the wielder of the pen on behalf of all the members of his particular group or syndicate. He would develop an instinctive knowledge and skill in the art of underwriting by which, over the years, he would become either a successful 'pen underwriter', or he would cease to be supported by other merchants and would fade out of his fraternity. A pen underwriter employed clerks who would record brief details of the insurance transactions undertaken. They were known as 'entry boys', and most successful pen underwriters started their careers in this way as entry boys, a tradition which has continued to this day.

Third parties began to specialise in arranging such deals between the merchants or shipowners and the underwriters, and became recognised amongst the groups in the coffee house as 'brokers'. Brokers had no personal insurable interest in the ships or cargoes. Neither did they put any of their own money at risk, except occasionally. Their income was derived from commissions or 'brokerage' paid to them by the underwriters for the risks they offered and their knowledge about the merchants and their trading interests.

The coffee house underwriters were dependent for the most

part upon information given by ships' captains who would report if they had actually seen safe arrivals thousands of miles away and many months before. Conversely, they might have witnessed or received reliable knowledge of various total or partial losses. They also brought back from their travels a wealth of news about everything of possible interest to the frequenters of the coffee house, which thus became not only a marketplace for insurance but also, equally important, a venue for mercantile intelligence of all kinds. Edward Lloyd seized upon and developed this particular niche, a very useful additional service which he was able to provide for his customers. His coffee house was a truly specialised version of the usual run of such establishments.

In 1691, Edward Lloyd moved to new premises in Lombard Street near the Royal Exchange, the acknowledged commercial centre of the City of London. Various publications were started, the titles of which contained the name 'Lloyd's'. The first, *Lloyd's News*, was not successful and after a short time was discontinued. In 1701, he started the publication of a news-sheet containing shipping information which came to be known as *Lloyd's List*. It grew from its origin as a broadsheet specific to Edward Lloyd's Coffee House into the newspaper still published today, the oldest daily newspaper in the United Kingdom. It carries general news specific to insurance and other general City activities. It also includes articles concerning various businesses, brief details of shipping, aviation, and casualties or losses, including such things as earthquakes, windstorms, and political upheavals occurring anywhere in the world. Another publication, *Lloyd's Register of Shipping*, was established in 1760, becoming a separate entity in 1834. Today, Lloyd's Register is one of the world's leading societies for the classification of ships and for surveying and reporting on other engineering enterprises.

There is very little detailed information concerning the layout of any of Edward Lloyd's Coffee Houses. From contemporary prints and the research that went into the building of a replica which was exhibited at Lloyd's as part of the Festival of Britain in 1951, the premises seemed to have followed the general pattern of the coffee houses of the day – but with certain specialised features. Not only was Lloyd's Coffee House a home for early Marine insurance in the City, but also for auction sales of many different kinds of merchandise, including vessels. Such auctions would be conducted from a circular construction known as the 'pulpit' placed near the entrance and from which the tables and high-backed pews would be clearly visible. According to the custom of the time, an auction lasted for the period that a one-inch candle took to burn. The pulpit was also used for news and important announcements, and there were notice boards upon which items of general or special interest to the customers would be posted. The pulpit subsequently developed into the 'caller's rostrum' in which the Lutine Bell was hung, the ringing of which preceded announcements – one ring for bad news, two for good. The bell had a chequered career, starting life on a French frigate *La Lutine*, which passed into British hands and was renamed HMS *Lutine*. In 1799 the ship sank off the Dutch coast, the bell being salvaged in 1859. The rostrum now forms the focal point inside Lloyd's underwriting room.

Edward Lloyd died in 1713 but his name lives on in the international insurance market today.

The Insurance Companies

The Monument, designed by Sir Christopher Wren, was built between 1671 and 1677 to commemorate the Great Fire of London. It stands 202 feet high and 202 feet from where the Great Fire started in a baker's premises in Pudding Lane on 2 September 1666. This fire developed very rapidly into a conflagration that destroyed more than half the buildings then located within the Square Mile, including the magnificent edifices of St Paul's Cathedral, the Guildhall, the Royal Exchange, the Customs House, many of the City Livery Companies' Halls, and dozens of City churches. Thousands of people were made homeless.

As so much wood and other combustible materials were used in the construction of buildings within which proliferated candles, oil lamps, open fireplaces, cooking and baking arrangements, fire was a major fear and concern for the inhabitants of a crowded area like the City of London. Concurrent with the emergence of Lloyd's as a centre for Marine insurance, various merchants and individuals were forming insurance 'companies' and 'societies', some on a mutual basis and others as joint stock companies, for the purpose of providing insurance for owners of properties against the risk of losing their houses or their businesses as a result of fire. By 1710 the best and most well-known was the Sun, which survives today after various mergers as the Royal & Sun Alliance.

Insurance companies offered not only a service of payment in the event of a policyholder having a loss due to fire, but also organised their own fire brigades consisting of crude, but efficient for the time, fire engines. These were basically see-saw double-hand pumps – horse or hand drawn. Together with his insurance policy, an insured or policyholder would be given a logo by the insurance company, known as a 'fire mark', to be displayed prominently on the front of his premises. Should a fire engine be directed to a burning building, and upon arrival the engine's insurance company's fire mark was not on display, the crew would ignore it and wait to be directed to a building that did have their fire mark on it!

The Innovators

After Edward Lloyd died, business continued to be conducted as usual until 1769 when The New Lloyd's Coffee House was established in Pope's Head Alley. Soon after, a group of underwriters and brokers subscribed money for the purpose of 'building or removing to another house for a more commodious reception of the gentlemen underwriters...' It was about this time that entry to Lloyd's was restricted to those conducting insurance business, originally referred to as 'subscribers', and where we can first find mention of a 'Committee of Lloyd's' which consisted of a selection of these subscribers elected by their fellows. And so Lloyd's itself became the property of – and was run by – the subscribers who arranged to rent space in the Royal Exchange through the intervention of John Julius Angerstein, commonly referred to by many as the 'Father of Lloyd's'.

When the Royal Exchange was destroyed by fire in 1838, Lloyd's moved to South Sea House. After the reconstruction of the Royal Exchange, Lloyd's returned there in 1844, being located in what became known as 'Lloyd's Subscription Rooms', and continued to operate as specialists in Marine insurance until the late 1880s when the first Non-Marine Fire policy was underwritten by a subscriber called Cuthbert Heath.

Cuthbert Heath can truthfully be described as the founder of the Non-Marine market operating at Lloyd's and is a key figure in the history of Non-Marine underwriting. He wrote the first Lloyd's reinsurance policy. He was also instrumental in inventing and developing the specialist subject of Excess of Loss reinsurance. Cuthbert Heath, in my opinion, does not have sufficient credit given to him as a true pioneer of the way in which Lloyd's Non-Marine underwriters emerged and now conduct their business. He was the first underwriter to extend the simple Fire insurance policy covering buildings and contents against destruction by fire to include the risk of burglary. This innovation rapidly developed into insuring the stocks in trade of jewellers and other merchants trading in valuable small items, subsequently developing into 'All Risks' – a misleading title, of course.

The insurance companies of the day were horrified and many efforts were made to have his activities stopped. Fortunately for Lloyd's and the general public, Cuthbert Heath sailed on, happily inventing new Non-Marine forms of insurance including hazards or perils which were acceptable to all who required them and were only too anxious to buy them. Eventually, rather than being enemies, insurers – both mutual and stock companies – and Lloyd's began working together more in the way of friendly competitors. This resulted in a sensible acceptance of basic Non-Marine as opposed to Marine concepts and understandings.

The principle covered by the word 'average', in the United States referred to as 'co-insurance', developed into a basic principle covering insurances on property. A simple way of explaining this is to take a householder who thinks that £30,000 insurance for his contents is adequate, as he believes he has no individual item worth more than, say, £5,000 – so why should he bother to give more premium to his insurer than the absolute minimum (or maximum – depending upon which way you look at it)? This is where most people come unstuck because they are unaware of the legal principles and practices which apply to the insurance business. These are indeed complex, and 'insurance to value' is a key factor.

The reader should take the time to list all the contents including personal items and clothing in his house, not forgetting the loo, loft, garage and garden shed. In the kitchen there will be cooking utensils and equipment ranging from a cooker and freezer to knives and forks. In the cool of the garage there may be a wine rack with a dozen or more bottles. A price should then be put against each article on the list. I guarantee that most readers will find that they are woefully underinsured. Another main principle of insurance is that the policyholder should be put in the same position as he was before the loss, that is, he should be no worse off and no better off. So when listing prices for everyday goods he will know what it costs to replace them in the shops, but he should reduce these amounts because he has had the use of the items for some time and they will have depreciated in value.

On the other hand, he may well have items such as jewellery, antique furniture, or paintings which will have increased in value since they were acquired. Let us suppose there is a burglary. The insurers are entitled before settling the loss to look at the remaining items in the house, and they are perfectly entitled to note that the insured person has a policy for £30,000 on contents. He is claiming the items missing as being worth £15,000, but the remaining articles are obviously worth at least £85,000. The insured person would then be deemed to be underinsured. He could only reasonably expect to collect a proportion of the proved loss as related to the overall insurance bought, set against the obvious value of the remaining contents. This means that the overall value of the contents at the time the policy was taken out must have been £100,000. A fair settlement on this partial loss would be 30/100ths of £15,000, or £4,500. In the same way, if the insured lost everything, all he could expect to receive would be his policy limit of £30,000.

At some time Marine underwriters began underwriting what is known as Incidental Non-Marine insurance. As far as the Marine underwriter is concerned, the expression 'Incidental Non-Marine' means that he will accept truly Non-Marine exposures as incidental to a large Marine risk, with the small portion of the overall premium being allocated to his Incidental Non-Marine account. As an example, if you owned a fleet of ships which you wished to insure but wanted to keep your insurances compact, included on the Marine policy covering the ships (which might be worth £100 million) could be offices on the quay (worth, say, only £1 million). This loose principle gradually developed into a loophole whereby some Marine underwriters were even leading purely Non-Marine business through their Incidental Non-Marine accounts.

Marine underwriters would have on their books many 'smallish' vessels before the development of supertankers and VLCCs (Very Large Cargo Carriers). Instead of perhaps ten captains and first officers and likewise down through the crews, it paid the ship owners to invest in huge ships. Only one master was needed with one set of officers and one crew to transport the same amounts of oil or cargo which previously required ten or more vessels. This resulted in a reduction of overall Marine premiums, and the Marine underwriters found themselves subject to enormous losses from single events. The *Torrey Canyon*, wrecked off the Isles of Scilly in 1967, was an early example close to home. Apart from the loss of the vessel and its cargo, the pollution was catastrophic to the point where the British government ordered the vessel to be set on fire by the Royal Air Force. At that precise time I was on my way to the United States, flying some 30,000 feet above the event which was clearly visible from my plane's port windows. At 55,000 tons or so, the *Torrey Canyon*, a large vessel in its day, was modest in size compared with the 260,000 tons plus monsters subsequently built. Quite a number were lost, costing underwriters a great deal of money. To name just a few: *Benge Vanga, Amoco Cadiz, Neiva, Maria Alejandria, Matra, Atlas Titan, Andros Patria*.

Concurrent with the introduction of large ships were the rapid oil exploration and production programmes in many parts of the world, including the shallow waters and vicious seas of the North Sea and Eastern Atlantic, which before World War II had not been a point of interest for the oil companies. The oil rigs required reached enormous values, with equally enormous losses to underwriters in the event of a rig's destruction. 'Piper Alpha' is one to remember. A Marine syndicate in which I was a participant had not only a normal line on the risk itself but also paid many more losses by way of reinsurances of other underwriters participating on the same rig. The latter participations are known as 'LMXs' – London Market Excess Loss reinsurances.

What was evolving was the reverse of the principles of insurance in which the fortunes of the many are spread over the misfortunes of the few. We therefore saw a situation develop where huge losses could be expected from comparatively few premium sources. The 1970s saw a horrible succession of supertanker and VLCC losses. This encouraged Marine underwriters to expand their 'Incidental Non-Marine' writings substantially. And who can blame them? Some brokers even placed 'Covers' in the Marine market for purely Non-Marine business, most of which were profitable. Some went even further and employed Marine brokers full-time on placing Non-Marine business with their established underwriting friends in the Marine market. The blind selling to the blind? I sometimes pondered as to what sort of row might have developed if Non-Marine underwriters had started to write Incidental Marine business!

Up to then Lloyd's had settled down with different classes of business being policed or regulated by the underwriters who were underwriting the greatest proportion of each class respectively. Out of this, various Lloyd's associations came naturally into existence: LUA – Lloyd's Underwriters Association, the senior and longest existing, looking after the affairs of Marine underwriters; there followed the NMA – Non-Marine Association; LIBA – Lloyd's Insurance Brokers Association; and other associations covering other classes – for example, Motor Underwriters, Aviation Underwriters, and so on. All these associations and the activities of their members were supervised by the Committee of Lloyd's with the benevolent cooperation of the British Insurance Association.

The Room

'Lloyd's Insurance Market' remained in a corner of the Royal Exchange until 1928 when its own imposing building was opened in Leadenhall Street. These fine new premises certainly deserved the classification 'A1', derived originally from Lloyd's Register of Shipping, though more often attributed to the insurance market. In the days of sailing ships, hulls were classified using vowel letters – A, E, I, O, and U – and numerals were employed for the rigging – 1, 2, 3, 4 and 5 – so that a vessel with a first-class hull and first-class rigging was classified A1 while one less good might be designated E2, and so on. The expression 'A1 at Lloyd's' became a synonym for 'The Best'.

The basic principles and workings of Lloyd's had changed very little in substance by the time I obtained employment there in the late 1940s.

The underwriting room consisted of a large open area in the centre of which was the rostrum – an imposing high circular structure within which, above the floor of the underwriting room, sat the duty waiter known as the 'caller' who would be a senior member of Lloyd's Liveried Staff. He would be wearing a red cloak in common with the waiters guarding the entrances to 'The Room', as it was always known. Above the caller's head was the Lutine Bell which he rang by pulling on a rope. There were other waiters wearing smart navy blue uniforms with red collar tabs, and their duties included running a messenger service throughout the Lloyd's building.

The caller would be approached from all sides by persons wishing to contact other persons within The Room, and each little queue awaited his attention. To assist him in this task, he had a microphone and as people approached him they would say something quite simple, like 'Bowring, Langmead' which was how I could be contacted. The caller would intone in a singsong voice, using the traditional name of my company C. T. Bowring,

'George Bowring, Langmead.'

If I was in The Room and heard this – there was a continual background droning which was quite unintelligible until one's own name was called – I would wave, probably with a rolled up newspaper or slip case, in the hope that the person could spot me. I might be studying the casualty board, or *Lloyd's List* placed on lecterns. More likely, I would be in a queue of brokers at an underwriter's box, gossiping about any and every subject. The caller was in contact with Lloyd's telephone exchange. If there was a phone call for me, he added one more word so that the singsong voice would be heard to say, 'George Bowring, Langmead, telephone.' He was also in contact with the entrances to The Room and, instead of 'telephone' after my name, I might hear 'Leadenhall' or 'Lime' which would mean my visitor was at that particular entrance. George Bowring, a dynamic force behind both the company's oil and other trades and its English and American shipping company in the 1800s, became a member of Lloyd's in 1876 which is why his name was used to 'call' the firm.

Surrounding the rostrum were rows of underwriters' boxes similar to the original tables or boxes of Edward Lloyd's Coffee House, but modernised to the extent that above each box was a structure containing records of the risks the underwriter had accepted and a number of reference books. If he was a Marine underwriter these would include Lloyd's Confidential Index, and Lloyd's Register of Shipping, listing every ship and yacht registered in the world, and showing details such as date and place of construction, port of registration and, most importantly, the classification such as 'A1 at Lloyd's' (the best). There would be useful bundles of small pieces of plain paper hanging on string, one or more telephones, a desk blotter, ink-wells, extra pads of blotting paper, and the underwriter's stamp which showed the syndicate's name and number and spaces for references. Together these represented the tools of the underwriter's trade – apart, of course, from his memory reflecting very broad general knowledge acquired and built up during his life, including a good layman's comprehensive grasp of basic law principles. Some boxes had an additional simple refinement consisting of a wooden flap extension which the underwriter might raise and invite the broker to sit beside him instead of having to remain on his feet. The smallest number sitting on a box would be just 'the underwriter' and his assistant, 'the entry boy'. Large syndicates would have several boxes grouped together with various senior staff to whom the *underwriter* had delegated his full powers of 'wielding the pen'. When I started, the smallest box was occupied by one man and his 'boy' underwriting on behalf of only five Names, whereas the occupants of larger boxes could be underwriting on behalf of one hundred or many more Names.

The underwriters and their boxes formed only a half of the operation within Lloyd's. The underwriters could not exist without the brokers, and vice versa. The underwriters were fortunate in that they spent their day sitting down. Those individuals walking about or standing in line beside the boxes would be placing brokers, claims brokers, junior brokers, and scratch boys. They were the liaison between potential insureds, or other non-Lloyd's agents and brokers both at home and overseas, requiring insurance from Lloyd's for their clients. Most broking firms, certainly all the larger ones, had their own brokers' boxes. These were very simple, quite small, with no superstructure, but with a direct telephone extension to the broker's office. They were available for the waiters to leave documents, etc., and for brokers to call their offices, leave their slip cases during lunch, or just to sit and think.

The end product of the business of insurance is paying claims. Therefore, in Lloyd's the broker placing the business was no more or less important than the claims broker whose task was settling claims with the underwriters. Some underwriters used the far ends of their boxes for the purpose of settling claims, whereas other larger syndicates might have an entirely separate fully staffed box known as the 'claims box'. Many influential pen underwriters started on a claims box where, from an early stage in their career, they would begin to understand the horrifying things that can happen, ranging from an explosion in an oil refinery, to the wrong leg chopped off by a surgeon in a hospital, which would inevitably engender a medical malpractice suit against the hospital and medical people concerned and, ultimately, a claim against their Third Party Medical Malpractice Liability policies.

Underwriters subscribing to Lloyd's Syndicates' Survey Department received copies of each survey undertaken by the department on their behalf. Qualified surveyors, employed by this department on a full-time or consultancy basis, would inspect premises of potential assureds to give the underwriters independent opinions about the risks they might be asked to underwrite. These surveys were very comprehensive and thousands of them were produced. Some underwriters who subscribed to this service kept their copies in files in the immediate vicinity of their underwriting boxes. Fine! But, human nature being what it is, one nasty smart junior broker spent his lunch hours searching for surveys of named properties given to him by underworld friends, in order to find weaknesses in access to premises such as jewellers' shops and places where large sums of money had to be left overnight. His activities resulted in a visit to the Old Bailey and a considerable tightening up of security around underwriters' boxes.

In fairly close proximity to the rostrum and caller were the notice boards upon which were posted among other things messages from Lloyd's agents, timed and dated as and when they came in. The Intelligence Department was responsible for posting 'casualties' on the casualty board which was specific to that purpose. The notices were coloured – yellow for Marine, pink for Non-Marine, and blue for Aviation – and based upon telegrams, cables, telexes, etc., setting out brief details of any given casualty. It was interesting to follow a marine casualty. The New York registered freighter *Flying Enterprise* was disabled off the southwest coast of England in January 1952. The master, Captain Carlsen, stayed on board by himself looking after his ship as best he could until a few minutes before it sank. The story unfolded on the casualty board during the whole of that day's business in The Room. It was quite an experience to watch this drama develop. There was an electrifying atmosphere and a huge cheer went up when it was announced that Captain Carlsen had been rescued. The day was extremely busy for the 'Total Loss Only' (TLO) brokers whose speciality was to remove 'total loss' risks from underwriters who wished to lay off this ultimate Marine peril. Captain Carlsen was later presented with Lloyd's Medal for

Meritorious Services at an award ceremony held in the underwriting room.

TLOs start to be placed as soon as a vessel is notified as a casualty or a potential casualty of some kind. It could be engine failure, loss of steering, shifting cargo, or simply having been reported as aground. If a Marine underwriter had, say, a £50,000 line on a ship for the normal Marine perils, he might wish to lay off, *at a price*, the total loss only aspect of the risk with other underwriters who specialise in writing TLOs. In the early hours of notification of a potential casualty, the TLO rate could be perhaps 10 per cent, but in a few hours this rate might reach 60 or 70 per cent depending upon how much more seriously the ship seemed to be in trouble. If the ship did not sink, the TLO reinsurers would be, as they say, laughing all the way to the bank. If it did sink, the TLO underwriters would pay the loss but would also have received a very fat premium for the risk. Conversely, the original underwriter would have saved himself a large proportion of the loss. A collection of the telegrams coming in about the *Flying Enterprise* during the day and the TLO reinsurances offered and accepted would make fascinating reading.

Adjacent to the underwriting room was the library, which contained amongst other things a wealth of reference books of all kinds which underwriters and brokers might wish to use. The library also had quiet corners with tables and chairs, where discreet discussions could take place or the contents of the library researched at leisure. A unique place was the 'Nelson Room', containing numerous relics and artefacts of the great admiral, including correspondence between him and Lady Hamilton. Lloyd's underwriters always felt they owed a great debt to Admiral Nelson, his captains and the Royal Navy for keeping the French and Spanish fleets at bay and making the sea safe for many years for the British merchant ships insured at Lloyd's. Several floors above the underwriting room was the 'Captain's Room' – a very pleasant restaurant, coffee and tea room – where business could be discussed informally, discreetly and in quiet, relaxed surroundings.

The basement below The Room, reached by two semicircular staircases under the rostrum, contained the telephones room and exchange, also a barber shop, a tobacconist, a pharmacy, a coffee shop with sandwich counter, and graded washrooms and cloakrooms for members, subscribers, associates and substitutes. Just inside the Lime Street entrance, but not in The Room itself, was a small post office. During World War II the people who worked at Lloyd's undertook two extra but very essential tasks. Fire-watching was the first line of protection against German incendiary bombs. After their official working hours, on a roster basis – or, indeed, whenever the air raid siren sounded – fire-watchers did a magnificent job on the roofs of Lloyd's and neighbouring buildings, with buckets of sand and shovels extinguishing fires before they could take hold. Also, many Lloyd's men, upon finishing their normal business activities, would go down to the basement where the necessary machinery for a mini factory had been installed, at which small items directed towards the war effort were assembled.

A couple of years or so after I started, it was decided that the underwriting room was too small, and in the north-east corner of The Room scaffolding appeared, upon which was erected a platform for one corner of a proposed gallery, which remained on appraisal for some months. This scheme was abandoned. The use of the ground floor of the next-door premises, Royal Mail House, was obtained as an annexe to the existing underwriting space and one could walk from The Room into the annexe. This worked well until it was decided that proper new premises would have to be built.

A really beautiful building was constructed on the opposite side of Lime Street on a bomb site which had been used as a car park. It was officially opened by the Queen Mother in 1957, and the underwriting room moved to the new building the following year. I cannot overemphasise what a delightful building this was. It had everything that was needed, including air-conditioning – unusual in London at that time. There was a large ground floor area and a substantial gallery. This necessitated the calling system being suitably amended. On the ground floor the caller, still sitting under the Lutine Bell, continued to take the calls for brokers personally. Calls emanating from the gallery were relayed by telephone to the caller from a waiter sitting at a subsidiary rostrum in the gallery. There were many telephones on the walls and pillars on both floors, connected directly to the main caller's rostrum. A person called would go to one of these telephones and give his name and the number on the side of the box at which he was waiting. Above each rostrum was a board which flashed the locations of the persons called. The 1928 room was converted into offices for the Corporation of Lloyd's. A bridge spanned Lime Street joining the two buildings at approximately second or third floor level. Basically, the ground floor was allocated to Marine and the gallery was for Non-Marine. Alas, in a comparatively short time – due, in my opinion, to an unhealthy proliferation of new syndicates – this building was also considered by many to have become too small to contain the underwriting room. In fact, not only had the members' private writing room been absorbed into the Non-Marine underwriters' area of the gallery, but the car park was also being used for underwriting boxes. Because it was down below and had nondescript colour washed walls, it became known affectionately as 'The Yellow Submarine'.

It was obvious to me and to many of my contemporaries who were engaged in day to day business within The Room itself, especially brokers who, by the nature of their general walking around and listening activities were the best observers, that this accommodation problem would only be temporary, and the market had reached a peak as far as numbers of syndicates were concerned. Also, there simply was not enough talented and experienced underwriting expertise to serve the number of existing syndicates properly. In my opinion, and in the opinion of many of my associates, there was absolutely no need for a new and bigger building at that time or in the then foreseeable future. Although the underwriting capacity of Lloyd's itself as a market would obviously expand by acquisition of new Names and amalgamation amongst the numerous small- and medium-sized underwriting syndicates, the temporary 'space problem' within the market would solve itself, assisted by electronic data process-ing which was just gaining a foothold at Lloyd's. These thoughts were also influenced by the way in which long-established insurance companies were merging.

Nevertheless, another new building was erected on the site of the 1928 building and its extension. As the 1928 building was being demolished, many of its contents were sold, including the solid mahogany lavatory seats. I was unable to obtain one, unfortunately. They were beautiful, those seats. They were so comfortable. They fitted precisely! On a more serious note, one of the underwriting boxes was presented and shipped over to Guy Carpenter & Company, the most prominent reinsurance broker in New York. The box took pride of place in their reception area.

Some people thought the new building was the ultimate in high-tech construction to propel Lloyd's into the twenty-first century. Others, myself included, thought it was a disastrous waste of money.

The new building had many problems, some minor, some serious. A typical minor problem: telephones, attached to the walls and pillars, thoughtfully placed for brokers or anyone else to use, had shelving upon which to put documents – but at such an angle that the papers slid off the shelves on to the floor.

More serious problems included, for example, the low railed see-through escalators in The Room and the lifts constructed of glass on the outside of the building. Anyone with a fear of heights had difficulty moving within the building, and this fundamental trouble was demonstrated to me most forcibly when showing a client and his wife around Lloyd's. We had travelled up via the escalator happily enough. Psychologically, it is much easier to travel upwards than downwards, for example scrambling up and down cliffs. So there had been no problem upwards on the escalator. Both my guests were interested in what was going on and in everything that they had seen. However, when I conducted them back to the top of the escalators to go down, the lady simply froze. She could not step on the moving stairs and there was no way that I or her husband could persuade her to do so. She was unable to get into an outside lift for the same reason caused by the escalators, and my visitors had to be taken down, somewhat ignominiously, in the service lift with trolleys containing debris from the luncheon rooms.

I cannot help agreeing with those people, both inside and outside Lloyd's, who comment that the exterior of the building resembles a vast petrochemical plant and has no architectural beauty whatsoever. The April 1989 edition of *Lloyd's Newsletter* ran a competition with a photograph of the building and blank slots all over the picture in which the entrants had to suggest appropriate titles for all the bits and pieces. I was very gratified to be awarded first prize.

Anybody within the Lloyd's community who happened to have an engagement to speak about Lloyd's, either in this country or abroad, was required to submit the text of his speech to the Committee of Lloyd's for approval – which was quite right and proper. On one of my visits to the United States I had been invited to deliver a talk to an insurance fraternity in Los Angeles on the subject of Lloyd's and the London insurance market generally. In the text I referred to the fact that no ladies were permitted to work in The Room either as members of underwriters' staff or as brokers or brokers' assistants. I explained that, except for the casual officially conducted visitor, Lloyd's was a male only province, and elaborated upon this by saying because of the close proximity a broker would find himself to an underwriter when negotiating his business, particularly as he would not wish other brokers in the queue to overhear his negotiations, it was probably just as well! I was asked to call upon one of the committee members who explained to me that it would be advisable to alter my text as the committee was soon to announce that women were to be allowed equal access to the underwriting room, both as brokers and underwriters and their respective staffs. I changed my talk accordingly and left out any reference to this delicate subject. It amused me some months later to see that some brokers had recruited quite a number of attractive young ladies to conduct their business with underwriters.

At times the working day was relieved by a certain amount of hilarity, frivolity and leg pulling. The telephone room brings to mind a gentleman in his very early sixties who was in charge of my company's scratch boys. His job was to ensure that his little team got all the scratches (underwriters' initials on endorsements) required for that day. He was careful not to be personally involved in any actual scratching, but took up a position in the telephone room placing bets over the telephone on behalf of anybody who cared to approach him, both brokers and underwriters. When going down the stairs, it was obvious from the aroma of the strong brand of cigarettes he smoked that this gentleman was 'on duty', and once in the telephone room area a quick glance was enough to spot him, in his unique brown suit, awaiting 'clients'.

A small group of brokers and scratch boys organised a telephone joke concerning the claims box of a large syndicate where the senior claims man was very precise and pompous, and those of us in the vicinity of the box were warned that it was about to take place. An individual went down to the telephone room, rang this gentleman, claiming to be a telephone engineer checking trouble with the line, and asked him to repeat slowly and clearly, 'I cannot eat my currant bun.' He did as he was requested, whereupon he was told, 'Then you had better stuff it up your bum.' The look on his face was worth hanging about for.

Some underwriters would have bags of sweets or peppermints on their boxes for their broking friends to enjoy. When feeling in need of refreshment on passing such an accommodating box, a certain broker was well known for dipping into the bag to take out one of the delicacies offered, even though he never showed some of these boxes any business. One underwriter, who had had enough of this, warned all his broking friends that the sweets bag was out of bounds. Our hero eventually came by, stuck his hand in the bag and, to his chagrin, pain and embarrassment, not to mention the amusement of the onlookers, found a mousetrap clamped on to his fingers. That put a stop to his piracy.

COMPETITION

So that's what goes on!

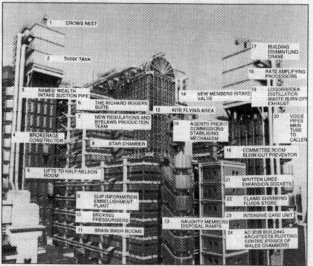

After much painstaking deliberation our judges have given us a decision on our Lloyd's building competition. In the best tradition of these occasions the results in reverse order are: second runner-up: John C Bennett, Grimston Scott; first runner-up: Clive Couzens, M E Warrington and Others; winner: Graham Langmead, who receives a magnum of Tercentenary Champagne. His winning entry is illustrated above and indicates the extremely high standard of humour of all the entries.

The Scratch Boy

After leaving the army in 1948, I started my insurance career working for one of the leading insurance brokers at Lloyd's, Willis Faber & Dumas. I was given no formal training, unless the first three days of my employment filing copies of insurance certificates counted as such. On the fourth day I was taken to Lloyd's.

All persons working in The Room, if they were not Names, subscribers or associates, were required to have passes known as substitute's tickets. My ticket was issued naming me as a substitute to the chairman of Willis. Prior to its issue I had to be interviewed by the superintendent of The Room to ensure that my demeanour and general appearance were of a satisfactory standard to conduct business in The Room (today this might well not be accepted as 'politically correct'!). I was shown the Willis broker's box, and where the loos were, and given a copy of a somewhat crude sketch map of the various boxes' locations.

Back at the office I was handed about thirty or so slips, each of which had a minor endorsement attached – cancellations, premium transfers (assigning portions of the premiums into the next year of three-year risks), and other simple alterations which needed initialling by the underwriters on the slip to which the endorsement was attached. Initialling is known as 'scratching' and after this initiation I was regarded as a fully qualified 'scratch boy' for Willis. The only other instruction I was given was that I was not on any account to approach 'the underwriter on the box' but to confine my approaches to persons at the middle or bottom end of the box. I sorted the slips into piles where each pile had the same underwriter as leader. Thinking this might be a good approach, I took my largest pile of about fifteen to twenty slips to the appropriate box, where I was received very politely and in a friendly manner by a young man who said, 'Good morning, sir. What have you got for us?' He took each of the slips, one by one, and solemnly initialled them. ('Sir', I discovered, was the form of address used by all underwriters and brokers in discussions with each other, no matter what their relative seniority was to each other. Naturally, as personal relationships developed over time the use of first names became acceptable.)

My next decision was whether to get the other leading underwriters' initials on the rest of the slips in my slip case or to proceed with those upon which I already had the leaders' scratches. On my first day in The Room it was a big decision. After two or three days I settled down into the routine of this postman-type operation, but I really had no idea what momentous transactions were taking place through my participation.

However, I was, as it turned out, to be extremely fortunate one morning to be waiting for a junior at the box of a syndicate called 'Rooper', the senior underwriter of which was Mr Joe Ballantine, who was sitting doing nothing. He motioned me to bring all my offerings to him personally, whereupon he asked me questions about each item, the answers to which I hadn't the faintest idea. He helped me make notes about his questions and told me to go back to my immediate boss and find out the answers. Upon my return to the office, I was instructed to go back to Mr Ballantine and tell him that if he didn't initial all the things I had in my slip case, he, my boss, would come up to Lloyd's and 'kick him in the arse'. I prevaricated with 'I can't tell him that!' To which he replied, 'I've known Joe for many years. He'll do what I say.' With some trepidation I returned to Mr Ballantine and passed on the message. That true gentleman got up from his seat, took me into the library and explained in detail everything that I was trying to achieve by the endorsements attached to the slips. This was my first proper break into the insurance business. At the end of about two hours, he told me never to come into Lloyd's again unless I knew what I was doing. I took his advice to heart.

Things didn't seem to be going all that well at Willis. A typical incident was when a senior reprimanded me for calling him Mr Smith instead of Captain Smith, as that was the rank he had reached in the army and was entitled to use afterwards. To cheer myself up, I said, 'In that case, Captain Smith, I think you should call me Major Langmead,' and immediately realised that this remark had done my career prospects no good at all. I was also getting a little depressed about my salary – £90 per annum was a great deal less than I had been receiving in the army. I was assured that £90 was good money for someone who had no knowledge about anything except killing people. In fact, I should be paying the company to teach me about my new-found trade.

I abandoned Lloyd's for a couple of months or so and took a job with a travel agent at a little over £200 per year. I hated the work, sitting in a coach in Somerset, reading to passengers from a crib sheet about sites and sights I had never seen before. Not knowing the territory, I had to concentrate on getting the expressions 'Here on your right' and 'Here on your left' correct. This was not for me.

The Broker

I headed back to the City of London in September 1948.

With just four months' previous experience at Lloyd's, I was now accepted as an 'old hand' in an expanding market and lucky enough to be taken on by C. T. Bowring as a fully fledged junior broker at an annual salary of £250. I had a new substitute's ticket in the name of the chairman, Harvey Bowring, and was assigned as the junior member of a team of four handling facultative reinsurances from North America.

When a broker's office opened in the morning, the staff – directors, senior brokers, junior brokers, scratch boys, secretaries, and others – would be busily attending to the morning's mail, including cables which had arrived overnight. The fact that London is east of North America made cable communication very easy. A cable sent from a North American office at its close of business would be available in London first thing London time. Conversely, a cable sent from a London office would arrive at an American office during business hours. In my early days, post departments would collect cables from central cable offices. Larger brokers offices had arrangements for bundles of cables to be delivered. There would also be bags of airmail or other letters delivered in similar fashion by the Post Office. Now, of course, it has become direct communication by telex, fax and e-mail, except for accounting and other routine business.

The morning's mail contained new orders, details of monetary transactions such as premiums, claims and brokerages, information about endorsements to existing policies, which could be anything from new acquisitions, increased values, cancellations and extensions, or other matters pertaining to policies about which it was necessary for underwriters to be informed. The telephone became important for clarifications, but was always used with the utmost care because of possible misunderstandings.

In the case of a new order, the broker's office staff – in consultation with the director or broker handling the risk on offer – would prepare a 'slip', the key document in negotiations between brokers and underwriters at Lloyd's and also insurance companies. The slip contains the type of insurance required (for example, Direct Physical Damage, Consequential Loss, Third Party Liabilities, or whatever), the name and address of the insured, the peril(s) to be insured, the period such as 'twelve months at 1 January', a brief description of the risk and any information which would be likely to influence a prudent underwriter in accepting or rejecting the offer. It also provides for him to quote or suggest a price or premium and to indicate the brokerage.

The slip is in fact the basis of the contract, and may be produced in evidence in the event of a dispute. This is important because it is tracked initially by the cover note – the first documentary evidence of cover to leave the broker's office, followed eventually by the policy. If necessary, it should be possible to ignore the policy and the cover note and rely solely on the slip to interpret the original intention of the contract agreed between the broker and the underwriters. At the bottom of the back of the slip would be displayed a reference showing the name of the source of the business, such as an overseas or local non-Lloyd's broker, and the date of the letter or cable by which the offer was received in the broker's office. On one occasion, this led to an amusing situation. One of our United States correspondents was a reinsurance broker, Guy Carpenter & Company of New York, and my team was handling facultative reinsurances from Carpenter's New York office. A Dutchman, underwriting for a Dutch insurance company in London, studied the details on the front of my slip, which happened to have been in respect of a large sprinklered reinforced concrete and steel office block, as stated under the information on the front of the slip. It was also a reinsurance of a prominent American insurance company which was retaining a very substantial amount. He casually turned the slip over and saw the reference of the American producer of the business: 'Carpenter N.Y. Cable 23 June 1950.' He fixed me with an angry stare and demanded, 'Vy do you hide ze fact zat zis risk is a *voodverker* on ze back of ze slip?' Some time later, the President of Guy Carpenter, George Nicholls, Senior, entertained me to lunch in a New York businessmen's club and I related this story using the required Dutch accent. He laughed so much that I feared he might do himself a mischief. Many of his friends ran across to the table: "George, are you all right?" With tears rolling down his face, he told them he could not do the story justice and suggested they all take his friend from Lloyd's out to lunch or dinner to hear it in its original form. I dined well during that visit!

A few old-fashioned brokers preferred to write their slips in their own handwriting, even to the point of emphasising the *good* and minimising the *not so good* facts of a risk under the information provided. For example, in the information on an unsprinklered risk the word 'sprinklered' would be penned in letters half an inch high with its prefix 'un' penned in letters one-eighth of an inch, thus: unSPRINKLERED. Another example: a tiny 'no' followed by a large 'municipal fire brigade' – no MUNICIPAL FIRE BRIGADE. Although this type of broker, usually referred to as a 'pick-up' merchant, was regarded as a bit of a joke, he wasted a great deal of everybody's time and was treated with scant respect.

Once a file is opened in the broker's office and a slip prepared, the individual broker's real job begins. He checks the slip with the file and it is his responsibility to ensure that it contains all the relevant information about the 'risk' – the common name by which all pieces of business are referred to between brokers and underwriters – and that it is a true summary of the offering. He then formulates his marketing strategy. This, primarily, will be to decide which underwriter or underwriters should be approached first. Although a small risk might be accepted 100 per cent by any one of several underwriters, as he has a large range to choose from, his duty is still to get the best possible deal for the insured, and he must therefore approach several syndicates to get the best quotation including the price and terms. To an experienced broker this will not be a difficult task, and his decision might well be influenced by such observations as to who is actually available and the length of the queues waiting at the boxes.

Just before the one o'clock lunchtime break, a queue of brokers would pull off a slip of paper from the underwriter's box and put down the initials of each broker in queue order. This ensured that after lunch the queue would be able to reassemble in its original form. Should the broker be negotiating a very large and complex risk with a wealth of back-up information including plans and maps, etc., it was normal to arrange an appointment in a leading underwriter's office away from the box. But in that event the actual line would have to be written at the underwriter's box in The Room at Lloyd's. Even with palatial offices, a Lloyd's underwriter's recognised place of business is at his box in The Room.

For a very special type of risk such as bloodstock, there would only be one or two underwriters prepared to write or at least to lead that class of business. On the other hand, in the case of a large risk involving many millions of dollars or pounds in values, the broker's first task will be to line up two or three of the recognised leads and obtain an agreed rate or premium on the slip together with the amounts or 'lines' that each of his leaders would be prepared to accept or write. 'Write' is a market expression usually used when talking about acceptances.

Upon completion of this key step, the transaction will temporarily cease as it will be necessary for the broker to communicate with the insured's broker across the Atlantic, or wherever, stating what he considers to be the best available indication. In this context, the London broker has to be sufficiently confident that, with his background market knowledge, he will be able to complete the order once it is given. The expression 'quotation' used to be employed but, after a certain court held that 'quotation' implied completion, the word 'indication' came into general use. The broker, having submitted his indication by one means or another, cable, telex, fax, awaits confirmation that the terms indicated are acceptable. Once his indication is accepted, he returns to work in the marketplace.

In negotiating the three largish lines to start his slip going, he may have had to offer internal specific reinsurances to underwriters, either on a contributing or Excess of Loss basis. To explain: the underwriter might be prepared to write a line of, say, 5 per cent of the risk. However, if the broker knows he can offer the underwriter, say, 50 per cent excess of 50 per cent reinsurance of his line at an acceptable price, then his lead line may jump from 5 per cent to 10 per cent. In this example let us assume that the underwriter's line is 5 per cent of $1 million – $50,000. If he is offered 50 per cent excess of 50 per cent of his line, he might be prepared to increase his line to 10 per cent – $100,000. He would then have reinsurance protection $50,000 above $50,000 on his line, for which he would pay an agreed portion of his premium received for the $100,000 line. If the reinsuring market is within Lloyd's there would be no difficulties, but if the reinsurer is an outside company then the Lloyd's underwriter will have to bear in mind, inter alia, the overall amount of 'non-Lloyd's' reinsurance he is permitted to use.

Concerning internal reinsurance of an underwriter's line, it became an academic discussion as to where internal reinsurance became pure 'fronting', and this could teeter towards dangerous situations in both directions. If the security of the reinsurance taken by an underwriter failed, then he would still be liable for the whole of the amount of the line he had written. Great care had to be taken by underwriters accepting and brokers offering reinsurance security that there should be no embarrassing situations.

Having sorted out those little problems and having had the three lead lines firmly written, the slip may now look healthily encouraging with lines totalling anything from 20 per cent to 30 per cent, and the broker will now have the long walk around The Room to complete his order. At the end of each day the Lloyd's broker reports to his producing broker or insurance agent the amount placed so far.

Here it is worth noting that on a very large risk the first line may be, say, 10 per cent placed with a big lead syndicate, whereas the last few lines may be as small as 1 per cent or fractions of 1 per cent. In order to save the broker's time, an underwriter might agree to cross off his syndicate number from the stamp's impression on the slip and write 'TBE' – 'To Be Entered' – which would be done later during the placing of the risk.

A curious but useful practice used occasionally was that of the 'Oblige Line'. A broker might have a small but most unpopular, for one reason or another, piece of business. Underwriters would not 'underwrite' such a risk but might be willing to help the broker out: fifty lines of $500 each would complete a $25,000 order. Adjacent to such a line the underwriter would pen 'T.O.' – 'To Oblige' – as his reference. Sometimes this notation might be elaborated to something like: 'D.O.T.O.T.D.O.B.A.' – 'Done Only To Oblige The Dear Old Bastard Again' – as a reference. For the fun of it, one underwriter kept a special account reference for such writings, and to his astonishment found that his loss ratios on such risks was vastly better than his usual loss ratios! Is there a message here somewhere?

Quite often, the broker may be offered a line which he considers at that time in the build-up of his slip to be too small to appear as yet on his slip, say, less than 4 per cent. A small line may be offered which is a disappointment to the broker, or it may be that he had seen an underwriter doing nothing so he pops in and picks up 1 per cent or 2 per cent as a 'promised line'. This was often written on one of the pieces of paper hanging on a string from the shelf above the underwriter's box or pencilled on the back of the slip. It was possible, and acceptable, to obtain a promised line outside The Room, which, of course, would have to be put down at the underwriter's box inside The Room, and in the days of absolute mutual trust between brokers and underwriters which pertained when I started business at Lloyd's the following incident will demonstrate what this meant.

In the very early 1950s I was short of $25,000 on a lumber mill in the State of Washington – a fairly high hazard risk – on a Friday evening. On my way back to the office I met an underwriter near Fenchurch Street Station. I told him of my problem and he said he would 'hold me covered' over the weekend. I cabled that the risk was completed. To my horror, amongst Monday morning's cables was one informing me that the lumber mill had burned on the Friday, State of Washington time. I went to the underwriter as soon as I could. I had nothing in writing. I said to him, 'Sir, you may remember agreeing to hold me covered for $25,000 outside Fenchurch Street Station late on Friday afternoon. I have just heard that the risk burned.'

His reply was, 'Sir, you'd better give me your slip and let me put my line down, hadn't you?'

A most important duty of the leading underwriter is to classify any risk which he leads as either 'Long Tail' or 'Short Tail', using the proper stamp for this purpose. Short Tail refers to those risks where all liability ceases at the end of the policy period. A simple example would be a twelve-month policy insuring against fire or other direct physical damage. It would be quite obvious upon expiry of the policy whether there had been a loss or not. Long Tail is used for those risks where claims or losses may not manifest themselves for a long time. It could be many years, in fact, after the actual policy period has expired before a loss rears its ugly head. An example is a drug which was administered to women who were prone to miscarry. This drug worked very satisfactorily and was of great benefit in reducing the numbers of miscarriages. Tragically, between ten to fifteen years after the drug was administered, female offspring of some mothers so treated developed gynaecological problems and the males various forms of impotency. Thus it would be many years before the insurance could be considered as finalised, or off risk, even after such a drug had ceased to be administered.

Once a risk had been completed and confirmed as such, a cover note would be prepared and forwarded. In due course, a policy with full wording would also be arranged by the broker. It would be signed at Lloyd's Policy Signing Office (LPSO) and by individual companies, if any, subscribing to the risk, but separate policies were mandatory for Lloyd's and companies participations.

The 'Lloyd's Market' developed into what became known by overseas, and particularly North American brokers, as the 'London Market', because of the sudden and rapidly expanded entrance of insurance companies, both United Kingdom and foreign, who wished to join the profitable explosion of 'Lloyd's type' business underwritten in London. In my opinion, this 'company' development was disastrous for many of those engaged in it and played a significant part in the problems in which Lloyd's found itself during the last twenty years or so of the twentieth century.

Naturally, brokers bringing business to insurers, whether they be Lloyd's underwriters or insurance companies, require and indeed deserve remuneration for their efforts. This is known as 'brokerage' and differs from insurance company's agents' commissions. The insurance company's agent is working on behalf of the company who employs or appoints him, whereas brokerage, although allowed by the insurer as a deduction from the premium, is earned by the broker acting on behalf of the insured. Very few insureds understand this subtle, but most important, difference as to whom is working for whom. Brokerage on an original (direct – as opposed to a reinsurance) offering varied according to circumstances. A typical direct American risk slip would show deductions from premium or rate as 'less 20 per cent and tax'. Very rarely but occasionally it might be '25 per cent and tax'. The tax was the State Tax, usually 4 per cent, and the 20 per cent brokerage was usually divided 15 per cent to the American agent or broker and 5 per cent to the Lloyd's or London broker. But, except for the tax, the amount deducted was always negotiable. Brokerage is shown at the bottom of the front of the slip.

When he became chairman of Lloyd's, Sir Matthew Drysdale, an imposing figure, used to appear at his underwriting box from time to time to keep in touch with the market. Sitting at his box one day, doing nothing while the rest of his underwriting staff were busy with their own queues, a young scratch boy approached him with a very minor endorsement – maybe a cancellation or a short extension. Sir Matthew looked at what had been set before him and said to the lad, 'If you buy a ticket at a railway station, you do not visit the station master.' From then on he was known as the 'Station Master'.

A certain broker, aware of the value of flattery, opened his conversation with Sir Matthew thus, 'You, sir, are a completely independent underwriter who makes up his mind without reference to any other insurer, are you not, sir?' Sir Matthew readily agreed. The broker amplified this. 'So you do not care what any other insurer does?'

'Absolutely correct.'

Whereupon the broker placed an endorsement in front of him and said, 'Then, sir, you cannot fail to agree this endorsement which shows that the warranted company has reduced its participation from 80 per cent to 20 per cent.'

Sir Matthew, without another word, scratched the endorsement. Such was the type of antic an unscrupulous broker might engage in, but he would soon become suspect in underwriters' eyes.

Another smart broker made a habit of approaching underwriters with three reasonably large risks, and he would place his slips in the following order: a good risk on the top, underneath that would be a not so good risk, and at the bottom would be a very-much-sought-after-by-underwriters risk. An underwriter would be happy to write the first, not so happy to write the second, but knew he would not be shown the bottom one, which would be the best of all, unless he was willing to subscribe to the middle one. This was known as the 'Three Slips Trick'.

I found that, as with Joe Ballantine, many of the underwriters with whom I was dealing were only too pleased to help me learn about American business which was coming to Lloyd's. They were happy to give me lessons about all kinds of things pertaining to insurance when they were not busy, in particular, Eric Squire of C. E. Heath, Len Durham and Bob Kiln of W. E. Hargreaves, George Price of G. N. Rouse, Julian Huxtable, Jack Cresswell and Henry Jeary of A. L. Sturge, Toby Green of Jansen Green, Harry Kraseman of W. C. Campbell, Stanley Lloyd Haine, Frank Green of Frank Green, and Len Toomey of Dick-Cleland. This was very encouraging and thoroughly enjoyable. With the assistance and personal tuition of these gentlemen, and many others, it was possible for me to develop and apply the general and detailed knowledge of the insurance business which enabled me to have such a satisfying career. Interestingly, the underwriters were far more enthusiastic about helping me learn the business than were seniors and colleagues in my own office. In retrospect, I was probably too keen and was considered to be a 'boat rocker'.

Having been welcomed back into The Room by underwriting staff, I continued my insurance education reading *Lloyd's List* and the insurance journal *Post Magazine*, as well as the American insurance publications *The National Underwriter*, *Business Insurance*, and *Best's Reports*. Fortunately, Bowrings had a very good in-house library of American and other insurance textbooks, pamphlets, and leaflets, together with copies of Insurance Law Reports. Meanwhile, remembering Joe Ballantine's advice, I had enrolled with the London Chartered Insurance Institute, received their textbooks, studied at home, and took and passed Parts I and II of their ACII examination (Associate of the Chartered Insurance Institute). The completion of these first two parts coincided with my introduction into all kinds of American business, about which the CII could offer nothing by way of education. So I decided there was no point in continuing the course. Ironically, many years later I was to provide the text for the Institute's chapters on North American insurance and reinsurance, for which the Institute declined to grant me even an honorary qualification!

When the team's work was slack, I would poke my nose into other teams' business and thereby began to handle some direct business as well as reinsurance. About the same time, I was asked to 'fill in' at a lunch with an American group from California. By great good luck, or fate, I was seated next to an American broker who asked me about insuring against the possibility of insufficient water being collected behind the dams' walls of a hydro-electric project on the South Fork of the Feather River in California. As I had come to believe anything could be insured at Lloyd's (such as Betty Grable's legs or Jimmy Durante's nose), I said that if he would give me some information I would study it over the weekend and make a presentation to underwriters the following week. He was highly pleased and after lunch gave me a fat file containing construction details of the project including technical terms, like 'acre feet' of water, which related to the amount of water necessary to be available behind each dam, for the project to go into electricity production in five years' time. It also had such things as rainfall and river flow statistics. He invited me to dinner that evening when we discussed the project at length. Having spent the weekend looking at the material and preparing a draft slip, I obtained permission from my boss to approach underwriters who priced it at a premium of $500,000, which was a very big direct order for a London broker in those days. The risk was successfully placed and it produced an interesting sideline.

The likelihood of a loss could not occur until the fifth and final year of the insurance contract, so dispensation was agreed by Lloyd's Policy Signing Office for a five-year continuous policy to be issued and, for accounting and signing purposes, each year the premium would be $1 nominal with the whole $500,000 premium to be paid in the final year. The only risk in this insurance was insufficient rainfall during the five-year period. The $500,000 premium charged for this risk was placed in escrow, from which the annual $1 nominal premium was drawn for the first four years. The balance, including interest earned, was paid for the fifth year. This small but successful attempt to put the bulk of 'earned' premium into the actual year of the possible loss was not questioned by any authority, and could form the basis of insurers' pleas to many tax authorities to allow so-called 'profits' to be reasonably carried forward until a natural catastrophe occurs, as outlined in the chapter on American insurance. The possible water shortage was my first successful individual negotiation of an interesting piece of business. Soon after the policy was issued, I was asked by the same gentleman to insure a Raisin Growers' Association against insufficient sun and too much rain. The grapes have to be dried in the open air for them to become acceptable raisins. As I recall, the premium for this was also fairly substantial and the risk was renewed year after year. Some might say this was like backing a horse both ways: to win and not to win! If there was too much rain, one policy would have to pay. If there was not enough rain, the other would!

A few months later Ian Skimming, the senior director in charge of Bowring's North American Non-Marine operation, who soon became chairman of the company, asked me to head up a team of four which he designated 'Special Risks Brokers'. Our brief was to help, get involved in, or develop any interesting and unusual insurances or reinsurances which emanated from anywhere in the world. His instruction was, 'Don't turn anything down out of hand until you have investigated the possibilities from all angles.' From then on things became really interesting – such as two separate Australian airlines which had an agreement whereby one leased an aircraft and its crew to the other. Both were concerned that this deal could affect their no-claims bonuses under their respective policies in the event that their leased aircraft were involved in a disaster. A suitable contingency insurance was put together which protected both airlines. Many other interesting and, indeed, unusual insurances were developed by the special risks team.

About this time, Bowring's Marine Department was aggressively soliciting American business and, under the auspices of a Marine director, put together at the request of Marsh & McLennan's San Francisco office a unique package in the Marine market for a Californian oil company, Standard Oil of California (SOCAL) subsequently known as Chevron. Basically, this was a policy placed in London with a limit of $100 million any one loss, accident, or occurrence, excess of $2 million. It insured SOCAL's refineries, marine tankers, road tankers, tank farms, pipelines, administrative buildings, etc., against all Marine and Non-Marine risks excess of $2 million. The $2 million underlying was either 'self-insured' or insured locally where such insurance had to be obtained, for example, Comprehensive General Liability, Automobile Liability, Workers' Compensation (known then as Workmen's Compensation), Products Liability, and so on. The policy was placed in the London Marine market but a number of Marine underwriters wanted to offload their purely Non-Marine exposures. My team – Ian Skimming's Special Risks Brokers – had the difficult task of persuading Non-Marine underwriters to take reinsurances of Marine underwriters on purely Non-Marine business, when Non-Marine underwriters were of the opinion that Marine underwriters didn't have the first idea what the original premiums should be for, say, a refinery. Between us all, this Marine-based package was successfully completed. It was the first of many packages, both Marine and Non-Marine based, which I handled on behalf of Bowrings.

I owe a great deal to the late Ian Skimming, who was my mentor in Bowrings. His untimely death was a great loss – to me personally, and to the company which had thereby lost the person who expanded it into the general financial world, and about whom an American friend said at the time we moved into the 1965 Bowring Building, 'Your company is at last getting into the twentieth century through the efforts of your chairman.' He was a superb leader.

Ian Skimming was also an inspired chairman of Bowrings. He guided it in its acquisitions and expansion to become a leading well-rounded City of London (and elsewhere) general financial institution which included, amongst others, Bowmakers, a leading provider of loans both private and commercial, and Singer & Friedlander, the well-known merchant bank. This great group was purchased curiously enough by an American insurance broker which had no interest in any part of the business other than its insurance broking activities, and soon after it was taken over the rest of the Bowring Group was dispensed with piecemeal. Thus a great name in British entrepreneurial history was snuffed out just like that. This whole episode was puzzling but not altogether surprising, and could well have been one of the factors involved in what went wrong (as discussed in the last chapter).

Lloyd's Policy Signing Office

Originally, the broker's office was responsible for preparation of the policies and for taking them around The Room to obtain a signature from every syndicate subscribing to the risks on the originating slips. This was a very time-consuming and laborious process.

The LPSO is a key bureaucratic organisation – in the very best meaning of that term – which eases and simplifies the complexities entailed in the preparation, signing and issuing of a policy which may have as many as two hundred or more syndicates subscribing to it.

It was a perfect marriage between the Brokers' Policy Departments and one of the underwriters' central organisations. It was where the discussions between individual underwriters and a broker reached fruition in a document for the insured or reinsured – a policy setting out a complex agreement between one party, the insured or reinsured, on the one side and a hundred or more syndicates on the other; but the syndicates, in fact, represented many hundreds of 'Names', each one of which appeared on the completed and signed policy together with the tiny fraction representing his or her participation.

The LPSO was moved out of the City in 1978 to an attractive building overlooking the Medway river at Chatham.

The Intelligence Service

The combination of ship's captains, the pulpit and the notice boards in Edward Lloyd's Coffee House formed the nucleus of what became Lloyd's Intelligence Service. This was aided by the development of international telegraph, telephone and radio services. Lloyd's Intelligence Department relied for much of its information on Lloyd's Agents who are officially appointed by the Committee/Council of Lloyd's.

Lloyd's Agents must not be confused in any way with *insurance agents*.

Their purpose, once they had been appointed in their own city, usually a sea port but not necessarily, was to be responsible for informing Lloyd's Intelligence Department in London of anything that happened in their respective localities which could possibly have a bearing on the fortunes of Lloyd's underwriters. Such appointees could be anything from a law firm to a salvage company or, in fact, any person or organisation not specifically engaged in the insurance business but likely to know what was going on in their local area. Production of intelligence is not their only contribution to Lloyd's as in a number of cases such Agents also act as surveyors and are even empowered by some underwriters to settle certain claims.

This intelligence service became so informative and responsible that in both World Wars it was placed under the government's own intelligence services. Some of the information produced was obviously highly sensitive and confidential and therefore, paradoxically, only available to the underwriters – who were paying for it – on a limited basis. To elaborate, it would be stupid to publish on the notice board at Lloyd's that the steam ship 'X' had been lost in the vicinity of 'Y', because this information would have been vital to the enemy's own intelligence service.

In a lighter vein, there was an unofficial but very useful internal intelligence service. Not to put too fine a point upon it, this might be described as the 'Gossip Service'.

> Celia: 'Here comes Monsieur Le Beau.'
> Rosalind: 'With his mouth full of news.'
>
> William Shakespeare, *As You Like It*, Act I, Scene II

General gossip in queues and to and from underwriters, as well as brokers in discussion with underwriters, was remarkable for getting a piece of news passed around the marketplace. An important underwriter, George Price, told me that if he wanted to get something passed around The Room quickly, he would send for one or two brokers he referred to as his 'Le Beaus' and to whom he would say, 'Don't tell anybody, but have you heard about...?'

The record time for something he started being returned to him was less than a quarter of an hour! George's intelligence service was based upon, first, there being only one secret in this life and that is something one invents oneself and never tells another soul, and, secondly, the human frailty of loving to show off knowledge.

World War II Developments

During the early months of 1939 it was becoming obvious that a major war in Europe was getting closer. By then about 50 per cent of the overall Lloyd's premium income came from North America. American insurance companies who were reinsured at Lloyd's, as well as producing agents and brokers who were sending direct business to Lloyd's, and individual policyholders, were all becoming concerned that investments held by Lloyd's underwriters in dollar securities, from which the American insureds and reinsureds would expect their losses to be paid, might be in jeopardy. A British government, being in dire straits to pay for arms and other materials essential to the conduct of a possible war, might decide to expropriate or nationalise such assets, which would not then be available to pay dollar losses or claims in America. This became so obvious to the sensible senior men at Lloyd's that a momentous but brilliant decision was taken to transfer *all* Lloyd's American funds – premiums, invested income, capital holdings – into a Dollar Trust Fund to be controlled by American trustees in New York. This could in no way be got at by any existing or future British government. Of course, in those days businessmen could take sensible and far-sighted decisions without the interfering dead hand of Brussels getting involved.

Every dollar of every premium paid by an American insured or reinsured company with Lloyd's underwriters went, in the first instance, into Lloyd's United States Dollar Premium Trust Fund. Losses also were paid directly out of this fund. This meant that every underwriting Name at Lloyd's had a share in the United States Trust Fund representing his insurance and reinsurance interests in American dollar business. With careful investment of these sacrosanct funds, Lloyd's United States Trust Fund grew impressively. Fortunately, this trust fund was properly established and legally in force before the formal outbreak of war in September 1939. It remains the financial mechanism through which American business is transacted at Lloyd's to this day, and is probably the main reason why Lloyd's not only survived but prospered during World War II.

After the war in Europe started in 1939, a problem arose concerning the fact that American insurance and reinsurance agents and brokers were cabling and writing to London for insurance and reinsurance coverages to be placed at Lloyd's. This applied not only to fixed properties on shore and liabilities of all kinds but also to ships and cargoes across the oceans. When the United States entered the war after Pearl Harbor in December 1941, the American authorities quite rightly decided to clamp down on *all* information pertaining to American property and interests, both ashore and afloat, being transmitted to anywhere in the world, including England. This made it almost impossible for a broker to offer business from the United States to an underwriter in London via a Lloyd's broker when any information concerning anything that was cabled or written about might be useful to the enemy. Such communications therefore ceased.

In its usual splendid innovative way, Lloyd's, together with the American authorities, came up with a practical answer. Experienced Lloyd's men were moved to New York where they set up a bureau to which all American requests for insurance were sent by brokers in San Francisco, Los Angeles, Chicago, Atlanta, Boston or wherever. Systems of numbers were devised which when transmitted were understood by the London brokers and underwriters but which would have been gobbledygook to enemy intelligence services. This was not a code as such but a reference system, known as BICO, and it worked. BICO was a small team from Lloyd's devised and inspired by the then chairman, Sir Eustace Pulbrook, the right man at the right time for the right job. It worked to the satisfaction of all parties – but, more importantly, it enabled American business to carry on flowing to Lloyd's, and, of course, the Dollar Premium Trust Fund had been set up in New York, which was already itself an important incentive to our American friends.

Some Marine War Risk premiums were impressive – but so were the shipping losses sustained to and from the United

Kingdom and America, Russia, South Africa, India, Australia, New Zealand, Malta, Egypt and elsewhere. Some spectacular losses occurred when U-boat packs managed to get within range of or into a convoy.

The magnificent transatlantic liners, the *Queen Mary* and the *Queen Elizabeth*, the latter only being completed after the outbreak of war, were requisitioned as troopships and did sterling service in bringing many hundreds of thousands of American soldiers across the Atlantic, in preparation for D-Day in 1944. Both these ships were unique, with speeds well in excess of 30 knots. This made them totally unsuitable to travel in a convoy proceeding at between 8 and 12 knots as they would have been prime targets for the enemy. They each, therefore, travelled separately at full speed. Fortunately, neither appeared in the periscope of a U-boat commander, or if they did and he had fired, he missed. They ended the war unscathed and were put back into civilian service. However, the *Queen Mary*, while crossing the Irish Sea during the war, collided with and cut in half an attendant cruiser, and there was sadly a large loss of life. No serious damage was incurred by the *Queen Mary*.

The insurance rate for the liners would have been specific to each vessel and each voyage, and very difficult to calculate on any kind of scientific basis. So it came back to a 'seat of the pants' type of underwriting at which, by then, Lloyd's underwriters had become very skilled. There is no way of explaining this except that an old hand sitting at his box at Lloyd's would always get a 'feel' for something, although in this case he would have had only two huge vessels upon which to exercise his built-in judgement.

American Insurance

Insurance in America commenced shortly before the War of Independence when Marine insurance was underwritten in Philadelphia at 'The London Coffee House'. Prior to that, anybody in the American colonies requiring insurance would have to arrange for it to be done in England.

The first mutual company was the Philadelphia Contributorship. This company issued fire marks and had its own firefighters. The Insurance Company of North America was the first stock company in the United States. The first completely independent insurance company was the Fireman's Fund on the West Coast. With the enormous distances involved a system was organised of General Agents who would issue policies together with all the necessary paperwork, including billings, collection of premiums, and payment of claims, which they would do on behalf of one or maybe several companies. A General Agent for all practical purposes was the company.

The regulation of insurance in the United States is complex, and involves first the individual state's Regulatory Authorities supervised by each state's own Insurance Commissioner's Department which licenses a company in its state for various classes of business. In any given state, such a company is referred to as a 'domestic' insurer, whereas companies incorporated in another state of the Union are referred to as 'foreign' insurers, while 'alien' applies to insurers which are incorporated in a foreign country. In order to do business in a given state, foreign and alien insurers have to become 'Admitted', thereby placing themselves under that particular state's regulations. A 'Non-Admitted' insurer, that is, one which is unlicensed within the state, is referred to as a 'Surplus Lines' insurer and, as such, must be approved by the state's Insurance Commissioner's Department.

Certain syndicates at Lloyds are licensed in the States of Illinois and Kentucky and also in the American Virgin Islands. All other Lloyd's syndicates are approved for Surplus Lines or Non-Admitted business in all states including Illinois but not Kentucky. People practising insurance in America are licensed by each state once they have successfully completed the examination set by the American Institute of Property and Liability Underwriters, which entitles them to the initials C.P.C.U. after their name – Chartered Property and Casualty Underwriter (also known, naughtily, as Can't Produce and Can't Underwrite!). Insurance in the United States, most of which is supervised by the National Association of Insurance Commissioners, is very involved concerning premiums and policy forms. Property insurance (Physical Damage) is fairly straightforward but Liability (Casualty) is very complex.

As far as Physical Damage, Non-Marine Fire and allied lines business is concerned, the policy forms or wordings are based in most areas on the 1943 New York Standard Fire Policy. This form usually includes an endorsement known as the 'Extended Coverage Endorsement' which adds the following perils to the policy: windstorm, hail, explosion, riot not attending a strike, civil commotion, aircraft and vehicular damage, and smoke. Other perils often covered include sprinkler leakage, subsidence, collapse, earthquake, flood, sonic boom, and landslide.

There is also what is referred to somewhat misleadingly as 'All Risks' covered normally under Inland Marine policy forms. There are many such examples including 'Jewellers Block', which covers most of the losses to which a jeweller may be exposed.

Most underwriters at Lloyd's subscribed to and had their own copies of *Best's*, a superb publication containing intimate and wide-ranging information about North American insurance companies, including their financial details and classifications or ratings of all classes of business written. This was a most valuable help to those underwriters who were writing reinsurances of North American companies and, indeed, for underwriters who were writing direct North American risks based on amounts being written by American insurance companies. For example, on the broker's slip might appear an order for $500,000, with the slip also showing that it was warranted that the XYZ Insurance

Company of America was writing $500,000 on the same basis. Occasionally, underwriters might be prepared to write the risk at, say, 80 per cent of the warranted company's rate because the underwriter's acquisition costs were less than those of the American company. After all, the warranted American company had already done the underwriting to its own satisfaction and standards which would be reflected in *Best's*.

North American Non-Marine direct, as opposed to reinsurance, business coming to Lloyd's was known on both sides of the Atlantic as 'Excess' and 'Surplus Lines'. 'Excess' refers to Excess Liability layers above primary basic Third Party Liability insurances, whereas 'Surplus Lines' refers to Physical Damage insurances which locally licensed insurers either did not wish to write or were precluded from writing because of their licensing requirements and restrictions. Small participations of individual licensed risks were allowed to qualify as Surplus Lines if only because the amount qualifying as Surplus Lines was being underwritten at, say, 80 per cent of the licensed insurer's rate of premium. Thus the Lloyd's broker's slip would show, say, a 15 per cent order based upon a licensed insurer's amount (warranted company's line) and follow all that licensed insurer's terms and conditions, with the exception of premium or rate, expressed on the slip as 'Full Warranted Clause Excluding Rate'.

Let us take an example. An American broker or agent is asked to place a risk with a value of $1 million. He places $900,000 with a licensed company at the licensed or 'board' rate (which would have come from the Rating Manual approved by the Commissioner of Insurance in that particular state), but in order to save his client (the insured) a little money, he would be permitted to offer the other $100,000 to unlicensed but approved Surplus Lines insurers such as Lloyd's. This $100,000 could then be placed at Lloyd's at less than the rate charged for the $900,000 participation. This would be satisfactory to all parties concerned, because the acquisition costs by the Lloyd's underwriters or by other Surplus Lines insurers would be less than those of the licensed company which would have to support the cost of its agency network, apart from as a licensed insurer having to write it only at the board rate. In other words, the underwriting judgement for that risk had been performed by a reputable American insurance company. Incidentally, a licensed insurer was permitted to write a given class of risk, say barbers' shops, at less than the board rate, but once having filed a deviated rate the insurer would have to write each and every barber shop offered to that insurer at the filed deviated rate.

Such regulations prevented the art of underwriting from developing naturally in the licensed American insurance market. They had the one dubious distinction of being non-discriminatory but, when one thinks about it, discrimination is what underwriting is really all about. In the United Kingdom a terrible driver may be driven off the road by exorbitant insurance premiums or even denied insurance. In the United States such drivers are 'given' to the Assigned Risk Pool of which every licensed automobile insurer is a member and has to accept the rogues in turn for the basic Third Party Liability insurance requirements of their respective states.

Marine insurance is mostly unregulated, but there is a very large amount of business known as 'Inland Marine' which broadly speaking covers the insurance of moveable property on an All Risks basis. Inland Marine insurance sounds like a contradiction in terms. It embraces insurance on all items of moveable property, and the wordings of such policies include language taken from Fire, Theft, Ocean Marine and others, but Ocean Marine as such is not included. The key requisite is that the property must be conveyable from one location to another. It is a very broad form and includes construction risks, bridges, railroads, and any other insurance pertaining to 'mobility'.

Liability insurance, known as Casualty business, is entirely different in its conduct from the way it is handled in England. Take motor car insurance: any driver who has a British Third Party Liability policy should be very content in that it is 'unlimited'. You will not find a limit of liability under the Third Party section of a British motor policy. Obviously, if it is a Comprehensive policy, there will be limits for the value of the car, medical benefits, and other extraneous coverages, but no limit as far as Third Party Liabilities are concerned. In the United States, in the case of automobile insurance, or any other Third Party

Liability policy for that matter, the insured buys a primary policy with what is known as 'basic limits', and then builds up excess layers above the primary with the object of protecting his assets against possible awards in the courts. The system applies equally to other Casualty classes such as General Liability (known as Comprehensive General Liability – CGL); Professional Liabilities of all kinds; Owners Landlords and Tenants (OLT); and Products Liability, probably the most volatile of all.

Most states' Insurance Departments publish their own 'Casualty Rating Manuals'. Such manuals are very comprehensive and at first glance very complicated. They list all types of risks showing the rates or premiums applicable to each type in relation to the basic primary insurance limit. They include debits or credits based on many factors: locations – cities, suburbs, towns, rural, and so on; numbers of employees; classes or categories of employees; turnover; payrolls. Classes of operations are numerous, ranging from hospitals to hairdressers, garages to livery stables, ski resorts to hotels, auto service stations to airport operators, etc. The range is almost limitless. Tables are included showing factors to be used or applied for increasing the published basic primary limits. The manual is the primary Casualty underwriter's 'bible'.

A British Liability policy does not differentiate between bodily injuries and property damage, but American policies do. The limits of a basic Primary Liability insurance might be expressed as $100,000/$300,000/$100,000. This would mean the insurer's liability was $100,000 in respect of bodily injury to any one person, $300,000 in respect of bodily injury to more than one person, and $100,000 in respect of physical damage to property, all being in respect of any one accident.

There are variations to this approach. Instead of 100/300/100, a primary Liability insurance might be expressed as, say, $500,000, or $1 million, Combined Single Limit (CSL). The CSL would be in respect of both bodily injury and property damage, also referred to as BI/PD. To amplify, our $1 million CSL might be fully expressed as $1 million Combined Single Limit Bodily Injury Property Damage (CSL BI/PD).

Having obtained a primary Liability insurance, an insured

could build up his Third Party Liability limits as previously mentioned in layers. There were many ways of expressing the layers above the primary.

A $900,000/$700,000/$900,000 excess layer would increase a 100/300/100 primary limit to $1 million/$1 million/$1 million. Alternatively, that could be expressed as the difference between $1 million/$1 million/$1 million and 100/300/100. Some companies express it differently from others, although it amounts to the same thing. Having established $1 million in respect of each of the original 100/300/100, higher limits usually went in straight multiples of $1 million. This sounds very complicated. And it is. Unnecessarily so. Nevertheless, it is the way that Casualty or Third Party Liability insurance developed in the United States.

A Comprehensive General Liability policy might or might not include such things as Products Liability, Occupational Disease (OD), or Automobile. But an Automobile Third Party Liability could be underwritten on its own without the inclusion of Comprehensive General Liability, Occupational Disease, and Products Liability.

Lloyd's came up with a brilliant conception, taken up avidly all over the United States, which was a form of policy known as 'Umbrella Liability'. An insured would have various primary Third Party Liability policies, each one of which would be written by state-licensed (Admitted) insurers using the approved rates and limits published in Rating Manuals by the appropriate regulating bodies. The Lloyd's Umbrella Liability Policy would sit over the top of all these policies as a further limit excess of all stated primaries. In addition, it also covers those areas where there is no primary policy, for example, libel and slander, or anything not specifically excluded, and these latter areas would be excess of what are known as the self-insured retention (SIR). All the primary policies would include defence costs which, in respect of most primary policies, would be unlimited amounts – but the Umbrella Liability policy would only include defence costs in those areas where there was no primary underlying insurance. However, an Umbrella policy also includes automatic replacement for underlying policies upon their exhaustion by losses.

Such a difference is very important when a legal dispute arises, as many lawyers appear not to understand the basic differences between a Straight Excess and an Umbrella Excess Liability policy. This was brought home very forcibly to me while giving evidence as an expert witness in an American court concerning the extent of the different coverages provided. One day, reconvening after lunch, the judge started the proceedings by saying, 'I think we will take Mr Langmead's impeachment next.'

I was completely unprepared for this and hadn't the slightest idea what he was talking about. It transpired that a lawyer had intimated that during one of the preparatory legal discussions I had contradicted myself in the afternoon on what I had said in the morning. During the morning session I had said that an Umbrella Excess Liability policy only included legal expenses in those areas of coverage where there was no underlying primary insurance. In the afternoon session I had said that an Excess Liability policy did not include legal expenses except by previous agreement between the Excess underwriters and the primary insurers. I think the reader will by now have realised that the lawyer was confusing a Straight Excess with an Umbrella Excess policy. A few questions and answers clarified the situation to everybody's satisfaction – not least mine – as the word 'impeachment' carries horrifying implications for anyone accused of such a gross misdemeanour.

The complexities of American Third Party Liability insurance have been explained at some length, because those of us who understand it often wonder whether the thousands of British tourists visiting North America and driving rented cars fully appreciate the difference between the insurance provided by car rental companies and the coverage given by their own insurance companies on their own cars back home – the latter being unlimited, whereas the former provides a basic or primary limit upon which as explained layers may be built up to whatever sum the prudent driver deems reasonable. It is not difficult to imagine the appalling situation of a British driver in his rented car, having bought the basic insurance provided by the car rental company, being judged the cause of a major freeway pile-up involving, say, two gasoline tankers, a couple of buses and dozens of cars, followed by likely awards made by American courts. When renting a car I always purchased many millions of dollars of Excess Liability insurance above the basic insurance offered by the rental company.

The accounts at the end of a year for both insurance companies and reinsurance companies include a most important but in many ways imponderable factor. This factor is the IBNR – Incurred But Not Reported – referring to losses. With property insurance this is fairly simple to calculate because an underwriter of Short Tail policies will know almost at once whether there have been losses. Has there been a burglary? Has there been a fire? Has there been a windstorm? And so on.

The IBNR for Long Tail business can only be assessed by experience and calculated guesswork. This will be variable. After an automobile accident the damage to the cars is obvious, but injuries to the persons involved may well not improve but deteriorate. Lawsuits for death or bodily injuries may drift on through Appeal Courts for years before the final figure is known. That situation is inevitable.

But what about incidents that have not even been reported because they are not known about at all? An individual can be exposed to injurious substances the effects of which do not manifest themselves for years, in some cases for many years, such as radiation, asbestos, dusts. There are many other issues which have only arisen during the last fifty years or so, such as tobacco, involving products which previously had been taken for granted but are now accepted as being dangerous to human health.

Another example of slow development which, as opposed to human sickness, concerns physical damage and related consequences is 'fatigue' in connection with metal, glass, adhesive or other materials. This is a slowly developing phenomenon which can be almost impossible to monitor or detect. It may reach its climax with possible disastrous consequences – serious damage, injuries or loss of life. An example might be a failure of a part, such as a window in a pressurised aircraft, which has developed over perhaps several years, the resultant sudden decompression causing the aircraft to disintegrate. Seepages and pollutions are other examples. It is very difficult, if not impossible, for anyone to pick on which policy year the failure or the pollution actually commenced, developed or occurred.

Third Party Liability or Casualty policies usually refer to 'Losses Occurring' during the period of the insurance. Unfortunately, there is a serious problem here. If an underwriter wishes to close his account, and he is wise, his IBNR factor should be many multiples of the premium, which is a non sequitur. Why? A reasonable premium received for a policy written for twelve months at 1 January 1960 would be very different from that received for a similar policy running for twelve months at 1 January 1990.

A policy written on a Losses Occurring basis during any given twelve months period can never safely be considered as terminated, and since the end of World War II this has been an accelerating problem in the insurance industry. The only practical way of writing such policies, in my opinion, is on what is known as 'claims made during the policy period' basis. Given the nature of the risk and all that is known about it and the history of the subject matter, it is possible to calculate or assess a reasonable premium to apply to such a policy. The use of this wording almost reduces the IBNR factor to that of property insurance, as the only imponderable – once a claim has been made – is how long it will take the courts to come to a final decision. There is no perfect solution, which can be demonstrated by saying that although 'claims made' during the policy period is a very good solution, it does not address, for example, the situation where an industrial or other organisation goes out of business and insurance ceases. In such an instance, a losses occurred basis would go on to extinction, and a claims made basis would be no good whatsoever for claimants.

The whole question of Liability or Casualty insurance in relation to the United States needs to be explored further in great depth; I shall start by summarising the five distinct and clearly recognisable factors, and then analyse them individually. They are:

first   no win no fee offerings by US lawyers (now becoming
             popular in the UK)
second   contingent fees
third   punitive damages

| fourth | and even more significant, and in fact the most important, policy wording '*losses occurring during the policy period*' |
| fifth | no aggregate limits – this is closely related to the fourth. |

Dealing with the first three:

No win no fee. This has been practised in North America for many years by lawyers who agree to act for plaintiffs on the basis that if they do not win the case the lawyer will charge no fee, and is closely related to:

Contingent fees, which means that before the case is heard the plaintiff agrees with his lawyer a percentage of the award, if any, that the lawyer will receive as his fee. In such cases a percentage can be very high, so it is only reasonable to suggest that a jury or a judge being aware of this fact and thinking that the damages to the plaintiff should be, say, $1 million, actually awards $2 million to take care of the lawyer's fees. This last point is equivalent to an insurer paying double the loss for the single premium he had received for a particular risk, if you think about it.

Quite naturally, as the public were looking for compensation, the lawyers were looking for loopholes to assist in the dogma which developed in the latter half of the twentieth century: 'They, or somebody, must be made to pay.' Unfortunately for the insurers, this has reached or is rapidly reaching a point where people who voluntarily enter into practices of any kind for enjoyment will look for compensation from the providers of such activities. So should a water-skier have an accident, he will seek compensation from the organisers of his fun, the driver of the speedboat, and the manufacturers and suppliers of the boat and the skis and the rope he was holding.

There is a well-known case in the United States where a woman, after bathing her poodle, put it in a microwave oven to dry. The dog did not survive this experience, and the owner successfully sued the manufacturers of the oven. Another woman lit a cigarette while she was spraying her hair, resulting in the spray can becoming a miniature flame-thrower. She successfully sued the makers of the hairspray. An elephant trainer successfully sued a circus in which he was performing after being badly burned by the elephant which urinated while it was standing over him. Of course, it had not been appreciated that the elephant might want to relieve itself at that moment or that an elephant's urine is very highly acidified. A theatre was sued when a man, after visiting the washroom during the interval, realised he wasn't 'zipped up'. As soon as the lights went down he tried to zip up under his programme but became inextricably attached to the flowing evening gown of the lady in the next seat. In the early days of pressurised passenger aircraft an airline was sued by a lady for her loss of dignity after using the lavatory during a flight in one of their airplanes. She had flushed the loo while still seated 'on the john'. The resultant suction meant she was unable to move. The flight engineer was eventually able to release her, inserting the handle of a large spoon between herself and the pan.

Apart from these examples, there were many other serious and inexcusable occurrences, such as the man whose good leg was amputated instead of the one which was gangrenous. He successfully sued the hospital: his damages were enormous, and rightly so.

It must be remembered that if insurers are successfully sued, they also normally pay the plaintiff's costs. The complication arises here where certain lawyers – colloquially known as 'ambulance chasers' – take on cases on a 'no win no fee' basis, but naturally if the lawsuit is successful they will have had built into their contract with the plaintiff a very large percentage of the award to cover their fees. This could amount to 50 per cent or more.

Punitive damages is another interesting North American practice which is similar to a fine but, unlike a normal fine, the proceeds are added to a court award and do not go to any authority but to the plaintiff. It would not be unusual for a straightforward award of, say, $5 million, being the actual amount that the court deemed to be appropriate for the injuries received, being increased to $20 million – $15 million of which represents the 'punitive' element. Naturally, damages and punitive damages would be subject to appeals with the law process, thereby increasing insured legal costs to the detriment of the insurers. The party against whom both damages and punitive damages have been awarded would still be liable for prosecution by the police or other authority, and this could involve a fine, imprisonment or appropriate penalty for whatever the wrongdoing was.

Now to the fourth factor:

Losses occurring during the policy period. This expression is certainly the most important and is very much more significant than appears at first sight. To a layman 'losses occurring during the policy period' could well be understood to mean that losses which happened during the policy period were settled during that time or shortly thereafter. Furthermore, such understanding would assume that the accidents were known to have happened. Unfortunately, common sense and reasonable assumptions went out of the window when long-term unknown damaging factors manifested themselves (with the help of a few lawyers here and there), and were seized upon as suitable grounds for making claims on the basis of 'things' that had 'occurred' twenty, thirty, forty or more years previously, and went on happening and getting worse during those periods of time.

Take, for example, a heavy smoker who develops lung cancer. Was this caused by the first cigarette he smoked or the 2,065th, or the 100,000th? Whichever it was, and the fact that his smoking caused the lung cancer could still be debatable. And which cigarette actually caused the illness? To complicate it a little more, if that smoker had used one brand for ten years, moved on to another brand for the next ten years, and finished up with an entirely different brand, and if it was established that smoking had indeed caused the lung cancer, which manufacturer was to blame? It is interesting to remember that during World War II every British serviceman (including myself) was issued with a weekly free ration of fifty cigarettes, and all films and plays had scenes of elegant smoking activities. I was visiting a university college in California whose insurances Bowrings handled, and discussed with the Dean of the Faculty of Medicine the problem of giving up smoking – I was at that time 'using' forty cigarettes a day. I was to be his guest at lunch, and before leaving for the restaurant he took me into the museum where there was a shelf of pickled lungs. They ranged from what appeared to be nice pink sponges to what seemed like sponges which had been dropped into a bucket of tar. A brief description below each container explained why the lungs looked as they did. That demonstration had the required effect. Back at my hotel I gave my entire stock of duty-frees to the staff, and have not smoked since.

Probably the worst 'normal' substance concerned in insurance claims was asbestos, which for years had been accepted as a very effective insulating material. It was easy to use, and appeared in many forms in the building trade and other industries. Asbestos-based sheets were used in partitions and for insulation. It appeared in brake linings in cars and simple items for the home such as saucepan underlays and on the ends of ironing boards. This commonplace material had been widely accepted as serviceable, safe and very useful. Progress being what it is, scientists, chemists, doctors, or whatever, became aware that asbestos was the cause of a horrible disease identified as asbestosis, caused by people using the substance either during their work or becoming exposed to it in some other way. The person who developed asbestosis is in the same category as the person who developed lung cancer through smoking, and the big question is, when did the incident occur that caused the problem? Was it when the material itself was being processed? Was it when the finished parts using asbestos were being manufactured? Was it during the cleaning or maintenance of such parts? Was it through a gradual unknown development or slow exposure to this new 'hazard'? The imponderables are manifold.

The complete farce of paying claims in respect of today's awards being funded out of premiums received anything from up to fifty or more years ago may be demonstrated by comparing house prices over given periods of time:

House 'A':	1948 – £17,000	2000 – £1.2 million
House 'B':	1966 – £35,000	2000 – £2.4 million
House 'C':	1967 – £11,000	2000 – £850,000

And this brings us to the fifth factor which concerns '*no aggregate limits*' and is closely related to the fourth factor 'losses occurring during the policy period'. When insurers were writing Products Liability, I could never understand why frequently there was no mention of an aggregate limit to apply to the policy, particularly a policy which referred to losses occurring during the policy period. To me this was tantamount to the removal of all liability from the insured regardless of what he was doing or manufacturing. The insurer might just as well have given the manufacturer a financial guarantee to do whatever he wished, which, of course, no normal investor or banker as opposed to an insurer would have dreamed of doing.

Thinking along these lines raises the Big Question. What other things, products or situations are we using or being exposed to today as a normal part of life will or could become liability disasters – air 'conditioning', which can be the simple recycling of stale air containing germs left in the system; mobile telephones and their attendant broadcasting and aerial systems; overhead transmission lines; microwave ovens; sunbeds; computer screens; beautifying processes; detergents; DDT; GM crops; hamburgers; plastics; noise amplification in discos and theatres; electronic screening in shops (remember Chapter I – The Test!) and in airports and venues where security is paramount... or even basking in the sun's rays inside an aircraft at 35,000 feet? Some of these examples are thought by many to be potentials for what is now widely referred to as 'ray damage'.

Having pondered that for a while, one goes back to the contention that the sensible way of underwriting Third Party Liability policies, especially those which include Products Liability, can only be on the basis of '*claims made during the policy period*'. This would establish not only a policy year of premiums from which the claim should be paid but, in the general circumstances or climate pertaining during that year, a much more appropriate premium would have been charged for the policy. To put it another way, it would remove the illogical situation of an underwriter assessing the premium for a risk many of the potential hazards of which he and everyone else is totally unaware and which will not manifest themselves for an indefinite number of years after the *policy year* had expired. This was described to me by one of my underwriting friends as being tantamount to a blind man looking through the wrong end of a telescope on a foggy night in an unlit cellar for a black cat that wasn't there! 'Claims made' is now the only realistic way to underwrite Third Party Liability or Casualty insurance, and it is becoming more and more recognised worldwide as such with the additional safeguard of an aggregate limit applicable separately to each policy year. But there is still a huge backlog of potential liability claims lingering in the background, some of which will come as a complete surprise to claimants and insurers alike.

Concurrent with the problems besetting purely American and Lloyd's insurers of American Liability insurance occurred the significant emergence of the phenomenon which eventually became known as the 'Weavers Affair'. Henry Weavers was Leslie Dew's deputy at Lloyd's. Leslie Dew was a very competent senior Casualty underwriter. During one of my early visits to Detroit, I encountered Henry by chance in the hotel lobby. He told me he was entering into a personal agreement with an American Casualty insurance company to underwrite Casualty business for them in the London market, and asked me not to mention this meeting. His successful visit snowballed into the large Casualty underwriting operation in London known as H. S. Weavers. The companies comprising this organisation changed over the years. Eventually, Weavers went into liquidation, being unable to meet its liabilities. In the London market, during the height of Weavers' activities, American Casualty insurance nearly always involved HSW, who was a major participant in, and in some cases led, large Liability insurances. Because of his Lloyd's background his organisation was generally accepted by those in Casualty marketing, although some of us had our reservations. Weavers' departure from the scene was one of the ominous signs for London North American Liability insurance generally.

When I retired from Bowrings, I was invited to become executive chairman of a new insurance broking company, London Special Risks, consisting of about twenty-five personnel in all. From being a reasonably large cog in a worldwide insurance broking operation, with several thousands of employees, to becoming the head of a new dynamic team was both enlightening and exciting. My first instruction to my new colleagues was that if they had any business with HSW, they should replace it immediately. Fortunately, they had placed only a relatively small volume with that organisation. This directive was received with dismay because HSW was a key market to all brokers. Nevertheless, my instruction was justified. Within less than twelve months HSW had ceased to underwrite.

As far as *property damage* is concerned, the problem is not one of IBNR but one of NYI – Not Yet Incurred (my own invention!). Perils such as windstorms, floods, tidal waves and earthquakes are obvious candidates. The premium for an insurance policy covering earthquake in an earthquake zone can at best be an educated guess based on the geological records, which are now very comprehensive. During my visits to San Francisco I was frequently told, 'We are well overdue for a serious earthquake right now.'

My first visit there was in 1961, but it was not until 1989 that a serious earthquake did occur causing a lot of damage to the city's infrastructure including one of the spans of the Oakland Bay Bridge being displaced and dropping into the bay. I also visited Los Angeles in 1961. While sitting in a twelfth floor office I became aware of vibrations and movements. My hosts, noticing my surprise, said, 'Don't worry: That's just a mini earthquake.' The next day's local newspaper had a headline in big letters: QUAKE ROCKS DOWNTOWN LA.

If there is no earthquake in any given year, then the earthquake premiums charged for that year would appear to have been excessive. On the other hand, if there is a serious earthquake in any given year, then in retrospect the premiums charged would be seen to have been far too small. The only way of rectifying this is that insurers should be encouraged by their tax authorities at the end of any given year to deem only a small fraction of the premiums paid for that year in respect of earthquake to be 'earned'. The balance of the premiums ought to be put legitimately into an interest-earning reserve fund. This theory should also apply to all insurances or reinsurances in respect of any natural catastrophe. This idea is akin to the insurance, mentioned earlier, of the hydro-electric scheme on the South Fork of the Feather River in California where no loss could possibly be paid on the five-year policy until the fifth and final year.

Another innovation which arose through American business was a very efficient marketing device known as a 'binding authority'. A slip would be prepared not in the name of a specific risk but in that of a responsible North American insurance agent or broker known as the cover holder who, once the Lloyd's Policy Signing Office had signed the binding authority, would be permitted to underwrite and issue certificates of insurance in his office on certain clearly defined classes of business. The London Lloyd's broker in the first instance would have to satisfy himself as to the North American agent's or broker's integrity, financial situation, and standing within his local insurance community. Lloyd's would also make its own enquiries via what was known as 'The Tribunal'. A binding authority was clearly specific in what was permitted to be bound, and was a very successful method of increasing the production of business for underwriters. There is no doubt whatsoever that a great volume of profitable business was brought to them by this method. There would always be safeguards for the protection of Lloyd's underwriters subscribing to this type of arrangement, such as exclusions, in respect of perils and classes of business, an annual premium income limitation – and, most importantly, there would be a substantial profit commission built into the binding authority's wording, which itself alone was a great incentive to the cover holder to underwrite good business. Inevitably, there were occasions when such arrangements were abused. All binding authorities in which I was involved represented a good slice of profitable business for the subscribing underwriters.

Another interesting insurance which developed over the years at Lloyd's is known as Excess Aggregate Workers' Compensation insurance (WCA). By law, employers have to insure their employees for compensation arising out of mishaps occurring in the course of their employment. Employers can be released from this obligation by posting a bond or some other satisfactory financial arrangement to take care of their potential liabilities. This is a statutory requirement. However, in most states approved self-insurance is permitted, and Lloyd's developed a scheme whereby they offer insurance on an 'Excess Aggregate' basis. An aggregate figure is agreed at the beginning of a policy year, and underwriters reimburse the insured (the employer) for any sums incurred over and above the agreed figure. There has to be a recognised service company involved to handle claims. Worker's Compensation is a statutory liability whereas 'Employers'

Liability' is dependent upon awards made in the courts.

Unemployment compensation insurance is similar in many ways to Excess Aggregate WCA. It arises from the Social Security legislation of 1935, as amended in 1972. Basically, employers pay about 3 per cent on their payrolls which forms the nucleus of the Federal Unemployment Compensation Fund. The options are to pay the tax or reimburse the federal authority for unemployment benefits paid to their employees. The latter option is where insurance is required by employers to protect them on an Excess Aggregate basis in respect of statutory reimbursements to their employees.

Lloyd's North American Non-Marine business developed in the fields of licensed, Non-Admitted/Surplus Lines property business, and also Excess Liability – increasing coverage for awards from the standard Manually Rated Primary Third Party policies to any limit which the market capacity could absorb and which policyholders might wish to buy. Concurrently a huge volume of reinsurance business of all classes was built up over the years.

Reinsurance

Anyone owning a motor car, a house, a shop, or a factory, who looks for insurance against untoward eventualities, that is to say nasty things happening over which he may have very little if any control, usually goes to an insurance company (often referred to as an 'insurer') or to an agent of an insurance company or, probably more usefully, to an insurance broker, or today may be persuaded by advertisements to use the telephone for a quotation in respect of the protection he requires. Unfortunately, because insurance is by its nature so complex, the insured often does not know what he really requires Only an independent insurance broker can properly advise him. The insured pays a premium. The broker or agent, if used, gets a commission. The insured expects to collect money should he suffer an accident or loss of some kind.

The insurance company issuing this original insurance policy, and many hundreds of such policies, will also require protection because for a number of reasons it may be unable to manage the size of an individual risk, or it might realise that many of its existing risks are located so close to each other that they could become part of one catastrophe. This is where reinsurance plays its vital role in the business of insurance and it plays it in a variety of ways.

First, is the sharing or pooling of all risks that the insurer accepts with other insurers who, of course, are basically also competitors. The most important and simplest method of doing this is by what is called a 'Quota Share (or 'Proportional') Reinsurance Treaty' whereby an agreed percentage of every risk which the insurer accepts is ceded to another insurer known as its 'reinsurer'. The reinsurer is bound to accept everything that comes its way or is ceded to it during the period covered by the Quota Share Reinsurance Treaty. There may be exclusions in the treaty so that the insurer would have to make other arrangements for reinsurance in respect of such excluded items.

The insurer may underwrite a risk which does not fit, perhaps because of its size, into its Quota Share Treaty(ies), in which case it might have to use what is known as a 'Surplus Line Treaty'. Surplus Line, in this context, should not be confused with Excess and Surplus Lines American business, which is the description of business that falls outside normal internal American company underwriting practices. To the reinsurers, a Surplus Line Treaty is unlikely to be as profitable as a Quota Share Treaty, if only because it has been 'selected against' – that is, not receiving a full share of the reinsured's business or 'writings'. In its reinsurance programme the reinsured may have more than one Surplus Line Treaty – First Surplus, Second Surplus, and so on.

Naturally, as an insurer underwrites many different classes of business, so its reinsurance protections will be arranged in respect of each class, for example, Physical Damage to Property, Third Party Liabilities, Motor, Aviation, Marine, etc. Having exhausted these basic protections, the insurer might have underwritten or accepted an individual risk which exposes all its treaties to the maximum amounts permitted and still have a larger amount exposed to loss than it considers to be prudent. To take care of this outstanding imprudent liability, it would therefore obtain what is known as 'facultative reinsurance' which is specific to an individual risk as opposed to automatic reinsurance. Such specific reinsurance is handled by the broker in the same manner as he would a *direct* risk, that is to say, obtaining appropriate leads followed by the long walk from underwriter to underwriter, with lines starting at, say, 7½ to 10 per cent and finishing with fractions of 1 per cent.

A slip in respect of a facultative reinsurance would have the name of the reinsured company together with the amount the company is retaining for its own account: this might be expressed as follows: 'reinsurance of XYZ Insurance Company of Seattle, Washington, which is retaining $5 million subject to Excess of Loss and Treaty Reinsurances' (more about Excess of Loss Reinsurance later). Should the reinsurance order also be for $5 million, the slip might be shown in percentages, so if the original insurance issued by the reinsured company happened to be for

$10 million, both the reinsurance order and the retention could be expressed as 50 per cent or $5 million. As all insurance companies have automatic reinsurance programmes in place, the 50 per cent retention emphasises this by saying, 'Subject to Excess of Loss Reinsurance and Treaties', as mentioned above.

The brokerage on a facultative reinsurance slip was usually expressed in one of two ways: 'GOR less 35 per cent and 1 per cent FET' or 'ONR less 10 per cent and 1 per cent FET'. 'GOR' was the Gross Original Rate, that is, the amount paid by the original insured or policyholder. 'Thirty-five per cent' referred to the total of all commissions or brokerages in the chain added together – original agent, reinsurance brokers, and reinsurance ceding commission retained by the ceding company. 'FET' was the Federal Excise Tax. 'ONR' means the Original Net Rate paid by the insured, less the original agent's commission and the ceding commission retained by the ceding company. 'Ten per cent' refers to reinsurance commissions thereafter, being the reinsurance brokers' commissions split between the American and the London reinsurance brokers. In my opinion, 'GOR less 35 per cent' was a much clearer description for the reinsurer to assess than 'ONR less 10 per cent'. If an underwriter was really concerned about the difference between GOR and ONR, he would have to enquire, and it is most unlikely that the broker would have known without making further enquiries of his producer or agent. I repeat, 'GOR less 35 per cent' was a much more open way of expressing the deductions.

A development of facultative reinsurance was the introduction of 'A.F.B.s' (Automatic Facultative Binders), each of which would be in respect of one particular insurance company. Some of these required each individual risk to be accepted by one or two leads, but many required no specific acceptances and the reinsured company would simply supply quarterly or monthly lists (known as bordereaux) of risks declared. The largest and most sophisticated of these was placed on behalf of the Factory Insurance Association (F.I.A.) – a grouping of American property insurance companies – and it was unique in that it had no individual limit as such, but each declaration was subject to a $50 million 'Probable Maximum Loss' (P.M.L.) worked out from proper surveys of each risk, which obviously would contain a large element of calculated guesswork. It should be emphasised that a $50 million P.M.L. might well represent a real full value of $500 million or more. The F.I.A.'s A.F.B. came about as a result of a disastrous loss at a motor manufacturer's plant in Detroit which effectively caused the loss of all transmission systems for thousands of automobiles on the production lines. The Factory Insurance Association is now known as Industrial Risks Insurers after it merged with the Oil Insurance Association (O.I.A.).

Occasionally, an underwriter might be persuaded by the placing broker to increase his line by accepting a contributing reinsurance (provided he considered the security of the proposed reinsurer to be sound) from, say, 6 to 7½ per cent. This would have the effect of making the broker's slip look better. But here again the problem had to be faced – and in such an instance, when does a *reinsurance* turn into *'fronting'*? The underwriter and the broker would decide that between them.

Further down the line comes 'Excess of Loss ('Non-Proportional') Reinsurance' which could be done on an individual risk basis or on a catastrophe basis (the former being in respect of one risk only, whereas the latter would involve many individual risks in one accident or occurrence) through various other sophisticated forms of reinsurance to the ultimate, known as 'Stop Loss'. Stop Loss is designed to protect the insurer's retained premium income above a certain figure up to a further given figure. Retained premium income is the balance of premium income remaining after outgoing reinsurance premiums have been taken into account.

Excess of Loss reinsurance works thus: an original policy may be issued for an amount of, say, $1 million. Excess of Loss reinsurance might be purchased for $500,000 excess of $500,000 in respect of any one loss. The effect of this is that the original insurer pays up to the first $500,000 and the reinsurer comes in on any amount above $500,000. An appropriate premium would be agreed between the two. To assist, a 'Probable Maximum Loss' (P.M.L.), 'Possible Loss Expectancy' (P.L.E.), or 'Amount Subject' (subject to one loss) would be provided. These all contained a large element of calculated guesswork and would be worked out from surveys of the individual risks, as already described in connection with the Factory Insurance Association.

Catastrophes may be conflagrations (such as the Great Fire of London in 1666 which started in a bakehouse, and the Great Chicago Fire of 1871 which, it is alleged, was started in the stable behind the house of Patrick O'Leary and his family in DeKoven Street when Mrs O'Leary's cow kicked over a lighted lamp on to dry hay); windstorms, tornadoes, hurricanes and cyclones; floods, earthquakes, landslides and tsunami (tidal waves); or any mishap involving a large area of destruction as a result of or following one event. Incidentally, insurers love to use the word 'tsunami' instead of tidal waves; it sounds so important, especially at lectures! Hurricanes and windstorms are usually given a name. Originally, they were all feminine, such as the disastrous Hurricane 'Betsy' in America, but for political correctness the weather bureaux now alternate between masculine and feminine names.

In many parts of the world, companies which came to be known as professional reinsurers developed and prospered. They only offer themselves as reinsurers and do not normally underwrite original insurance risks, although some may do so. They are usually very large and regarded by many as fallback financial institutions rather than as insurers in the true meaning of the term. They do not require a large branch office and/or agency system as such, but more often than not occupy impressive premises. A knowledgeable and competent team of executives travel busily from one original insurer to another, drumming up or servicing business in a very professional manner.

An insurer ceding business to a reinsurer would expect to receive a payment for so doing. Provision would always be made in the reinsurance agreement for the reinsured to receive by way of consideration a ceding commission generally referred to as an over rider. In addition, a profit commission might be arranged to take care of the business ceded resulting in a profit to the reinsurer. An interesting Excess of Loss Reinsurance known as a Burning Cost, or Carpenter Plan ('CARPLAN') named after the American reinsurance broker, Guy Carpenter (mentioned earlier): all losses above the attaching point, or underlying limit, and up to the reinsurance limit incurred by the company would be aggregated for each of the preceding three, five or seven years, and an average struck which would be loaded by 100/70ths (sometimes 100/65ths). The resulting figure would be the first year's premium on a three-year, five-year or continuous contract. Thereafter, the formula would remain on an 'add a year, drop a year basis'. Of course, brokerage would be deducted from each year's premium.

For legal reasons it might be necessary in some countries for a local company to issue the original policy but with 100 per cent reinsurance in London, in which case such a company would be referred to as a 'fronting company'. The premium would have to be increased so that the fronting company was not out of pocket on expenses but made a modest profit by way of 'reinsurance commission'. Again, it must be emphasised that whoever issues the original policy is entirely responsible to the policyholder for any claims against it.

There were many large risks, that is, highly valued risks, which were underwritten on Inland Marine forms covering to all intents and purposes 'All Risks', and the American and United Kingdom insurance authorities listed and designated them as 'Target Risks'. Examples would be bridges, tunnels, fine art collections, and the like, that is to say high values on All Risks bases. A risk designated as a Target Risk was only permitted to be underwritten on a Net Line basis. An underwriter (or company) subscribing to such a named risk was not permitted to use any of his reinsurance facilities. All reinsurance programmes of any kind had a Target Risk Exclusion Clause in their policy wording. Typical examples are the Mellon Art Collection, bridges in the San Francisco Bay area such as the Golden Gate, San Francisco–Oakland Bay, San Mateo–Hayward, and on the other side of the continent the New York Port Authorities bridges and tunnels. The bridges in the San Francisco area, of course, are all located in close proximity to the various earthquake faults, especially the major San Andreas fault running north to south.

All the foregoing comments regarding reinsurances of insurance companies naturally apply equally to individual underwriting syndicates at Lloyd's.

Soon after I started my career at Lloyd's as a scratchboy, I met

Frank Barber, who was starting his career as an entry boy, sitting in the middle of one side of a box known as T.N.F. This was an unusual box in that it had two equally senior underwriters who sat opposite each other at one end, and Frank was kept very busy entering the risks which had been written by his two masters. He eventually became the underwriter on a box occupied by the syndicate known as W. D. Denham, which subsequently became Frank Barber and Others.

Frank, now enjoying his retirement in the country, was a truly brilliant underwriter. He had an exceptional flair with his reinsurances, and it was notable if I offered him a line on a 'package' policy which he might have considered to be underpriced, he would invariably ask me to come back in a couple of days to discuss it further with him. During those two days, he would arrange reinsurances of the package through various brokers, which would place his Names in a very favourable position. It didn't take the brokers long to coin the friendly sobriquet, 'Money in the bank, Frank.' He was very astute in his choice of reinsurance brokers and what he asked them to achieve. Frank was a real underwriting character of the old school, and truly deserved his success and his election as a deputy chairman of Lloyd's.

The Traveller

During the 1950s a Treaty broker would be privileged to accompany a Treaty director on his visits to big reinsurance accounts. He was euphemistically known as the 'bag carrier'. The chosen one would be seen busily checking that his boat train reservation to Southampton had been secured, as had his first-class accommodation on the *Queen Mary* or *Queen Elizabeth* to New York; that his bank account with the Midland Bank on the ship for £50 was secure, and his deckchair had been booked on the after-deck, etc. Not being a treaty broker, I never experienced this assisted initiation to travel.

The visits of Ian Skimming, chairman of Bowring's, to North America in those days were known colloquially as 'swings', as indeed were all visits by Bowring's representatives. Ian was a most remarkable post-World War II insurance and general financial wizard, and under his guidance Bowring expanded at a pace. I enjoyed listening to his views on all kinds of financial subjects, including his suggestion at lunch to British Rail that they should sell the main line stations in London to commercial interests who would redevelop the stations with office blocks above them and modernise the facilities for both commuters and long-distance travellers. That was just one of his ideas. On another occasion, when the chairman of an American reinsurance broker asked him what he would do if he [the American reinsurance broker] set up an office in London, Ian's reply was 'I'd cross the Atlantic and take over your parent company!' He acquired amongst others Bowmaker, the hire purchase and heavy plant hire company, and Singer and Friedlander, the merchant bank.

The purpose of the swings was threefold – first, to service existing accounts; second, to develop new business from existing accounts; and third, to open up new accounts. By 'accounts' is meant sources of business in North America which Bowrings in London could offer to the Lloyd's markets. Information about any proposed swing would be circulated to all departments in the company and the traveller would draw up a plan for the trip, having made sure that key individuals would be available on the dates of proposed important visits. The plan had, of necessity, to be capable of adaptation or alteration right up to departure and, indeed, during the trip itself. A typical swing would be New York, Boston, Miami, Houston, Atlanta, Los Angeles, San Francisco, Seattle, Toronto and Montreal.

Bowrings always used North American reinsurance brokers, known as reinsurance intermediaries, for its North American reinsurance business – with the exception of two large accounts, the Fireman's Fund Insurance Company and the St Paul Fire and Marine Insurance Company, both of which had been handled directly by Bowrings for many years. During Ian's swing in April 1961, the San Francisco office of Marsh & McLennan had expressed dissatisfaction about the capacity in the London market available for the insurances on the Golden Gate Bridge. Also, Fireman's Fund Insurance Company were concerned that not enough people in Bowrings, if any, understood direct Surplus Lines and Excess Liability business. He offered to send them a Bowring man for a few weeks.

One Thursday afternoon, on returning to the office from Lloyd's I found two messages, one from each of two directors asking me to see them. The secretary of the first said he'd gone home. The second was still there. His opening comment was, 'Ah, good. Graham, read these papers, and when you see Ian Skimming in Seattle on Sunday he'll bring you up to date.'

Totally nonplussed, I discovered that each director thought the other had been keeping me informed of events. In fact, neither of them had. When it was established that I was in total ignorance of what was going on, he handed me a file of cables covering the preceding two weeks, during which Ian was organising with his colleagues in London for me to join him on the West Coast of the United States in an endeavour to increase the insurance on the Golden Gate Bridge in San Francisco, and to introduce me to the Excess and Special Risks operation of the Fireman's Fund Insurance Company. Friday was frankly frenetic. An American visa had to be arranged and airline tickets and hotels booked. The only way to get to Seattle by Sunday was on Saturday's Air Canada flight from Heathrow to Vancouver, stopping at Prestwick, Montreal, Toronto, Winnipeg, Regina, and Calgary, and then by train on the Sunday morning from Vancouver to Seattle.

This journey was memorable. A Canadian lady sitting beside me on the plane mentioned that she and her husband had just bought an hotel in the West Indies which had been struck by a hurricane, and they were involved in negotiations with their insurers because of an interesting situation. The hotel was very severely damaged. In fact, it was almost a total loss. But there was a watercourse running beside the hotel which had brought down an enormous amount of rubble and soil from the hills above. This was spread out on the beach in front of the hotel in an arc. By rapidly revetting this rubble, their waterfront, instead of being a comparatively short straight stretch of beach, had become a large semicircle four or five times longer than the original frontage. Thus, the whole hotel complex was now worth very much more than it had been before the storm. So the owners' overall financial gain was far greater than the costs of the repairs to the hotel. I never did hear how that loss was finally settled – or 'adjusted', to use insurance jargon.

The first-class section of the early Air Canada Douglas DC8s was a delight. In front of the normal two-by-two seating was an area with small tables and chairs, and a fully equipped bar where one could chat and drink. In those days, all domestic, or internal, flights in Canada were 'dry'. However, this didn't apply to international passengers on continuing flights. As we approached Montreal, the senior air hostess said that as we were coming into Canadian airspace the bar was about to be closed. Knowing I was continuing to the West Coast and would be able to imbibe all the way to Vancouver, she suggested it would be a good idea to order two or three bottles of my favourite tipple before the bar shutter came down. She commented, with a twinkle in her eye, 'You'll be *very* popular!'

After clearing Customs and Immigration at Montreal, I returned to my seat to find I was the only passenger left, and the bar had disappeared rather like an American speakeasy in the days of Prohibition. A little while later, four or five Canadian businessmen, two of whom were senior executives of Caterpillar Tractor, boarded the plane. One of them enquired whether I had come from London. On hearing that I had, he asked, 'Did the girl tell you?' 'Do you mean about the booze?' 'Yes,' he said. As soon as we took off, three bottles of Scotch were delivered to me. A merry time was had by all and, being first class, it was free. I think. I can't clearly remember because when the plane touched down in Vancouver at midnight local time I had been travelling for more than twenty-four hours and had had very stimulating conversations with my new Canadian friends, not to mention those over the Atlantic. I gratefully checked into the hotel, fell into bed, and slept.

The train journey to Seattle passed peacefully enough, but on arrival I had to deal with unbelieving American Customs and Immigration officials who found it difficult to accept that a British businessman was making his first visit to the United States on a Sunday by train from Vancouver, having left London only the previous day!

Ian Skimming met me at the station, none too pleased to hear that I had not been kept informed about his cables and phone calls to his fellow directors. He gave me a briefing about the Golden Gate Bridge problem and Fireman's Fund's Excess and Special Risks Department before seeing me off at the airport for the flight down to San Francisco. When I look back upon all my business trips to North America, this first visit was one of the most interesting and illuminating.

The Golden Gate Bridge after completion was dedicated on 27 May 1937. It is one of what are known as target risks where all insurers write the risk on a purely Net Line basis without involving reinsurance in any way. The insurances on the bridge were designed primarily to protect the bondholders' annual interest payments on the bond, which was floated to finance the bridge's construction and operation, as there would not have been enough insurance in the world to pay for the replacement of the structure should it be severely damaged or destroyed. The issue of bonds is a standard sensible American practice on large-scale construction projects. At that time, $35 million was a heavy amount of insurance on one risk in a known earthquake area. My mission was to learn enough about the bridge to persuade underwriters to increase their Net Line participations. The Marsh & McLennan office in San Francisco arranged with the Golden Gate Bridge & Highway District Authority to show me all. This entailed riding to the top of the bridge in a small lift inside one of the two large tubes forming the south tower supporting the suspension cables, plus a scramble up a ladder to the flashing aircraft beacon. From there was to be had a breathtaking view of San Francisco, the Bay, Alcatraz, and the Oakland Bay shoreline. We then descended and inspected the foundations where measurements were constantly being recorded of earth movements.

The next day, at the Pacific Earthquake Rating Bureau, Professor Steinbrugge, a geologist and world expert on the subject of earthquakes, explained fascinating things – such as, a brick construction on solid rock in the vicinity of a fault could be expected to tumble down, whereas a single-storey wooden building on a reinforced concrete slab on soft ground would probably hold up. A steel frame skyscraper on solid rock fairly close to a fault would probably be secure, but if the shock was severe enough tall buildings far away could possibly bang and rattle together, like reeds in the wind, because the shock waves at the epicentre are violent for a short period but as they spread outwards, like ripples on a pond, they get larger and longer. All this was demonstrated with models, photographs and relief maps. The fault lines in California are so obvious on the ground, particularly the San Andreas Fault.

Having received an incredible amount of geological and engineering facts about earthquakes in relation to the region's bridges and other construction projects, I was able to discuss my experience with underwriters. As a result, on the next renewal the insurances were increased to $65 million, nearly double the previous figure.

During this trip, I spent a lot of time with Garry Redmond and his small team who underwrote for the Fireman's Fund's wide-ranging and profitable Excess and Special Risks Department, their in-house Surplus Lines operation. This was where I really started to understand the fundamentals of the American Non-Marine insurance business. Garry was my mentor in the basic complexities of American insurance, and provided me with textbooks of his company's in-house study programme. Upon returning home I eventually completed my answers to the examination questions, and sent them to the Fireman's Fund who advised me that I had passed. I first met Garry when he was the underwriter for an Irish insurance company in London, the Emerald, underwriting what was known as Lloyd's 'fringe type' business. He had been invited by the Fireman's Fund to be the underwriter for their Excess and Surplus Lines operation, which was underwriting similar business within the United States to that which Lloyd's underwriters were writing in London. This is a good example of the way the insurance business was and still is a comparatively small 'club'. Garry has retired to raise bloodstock in Kentucky.

Fireman's Fund Insurance Company, Marsh & McLennan, and other brokers I visited in California during this initial trip, including George Walker of Los Angeles, were all good business producers for Bowrings.

The journey home was not without interest. In those days a business visitor to the United States had to obtain clearance from the Inland Revenue and Immigration Authorities in the city from which he departed. This necessitated taking an overnight flight from San Francisco to New York where I checked into the Gladstone Hotel at about seven thirty in the morning. The Gladstone was Bowrings' usual New York domain. It was a splendid old-fashioned hotel. The luxurious bedrooms even had independent air-conditioning units attached to the outside of the windows.

The flight to London from Idlewild (now Kennedy) Airport was not until ten o'clock in the evening. I cleared the Internal Revenue Service offices by about nine that morning so the rest of the day was mine to discover New York. I flagged down a cab and explained to the driver that this was my first visit. He gave me The Tour (his). He took me to many places of interest and we had lunch together in a dinette off Wall Street. It transpired that we had both served very close to each other during the Italian campaign in World War II. On returning to the hotel he at first refused to take any payment because he had regarded that morning, as he put it, to have been an enjoyable holiday.

The Gladstone had a discreet dining room and an even more discreet bar. Still having a whole afternoon to kill, I looked in. At the far corner of the bar was a very distinguished-looking gentleman in deep conversation with a younger man and woman in what seemed to be a semi-serious questions and answers session, and they were easy to overhear. There was no one else present but the bartender who told me, when the party had left, that the elderly gentleman was Ernest Hemingway being interviewed for a magazine. It was a fascinating couple of hours which I shall never forget. A few months later the great man was dead.

The beautiful old Gladstone was eventually pulled down to make way for a large modern hotel.

Swings and Risks

My next trip was to accompany a senior director, Keith Batchelor, on a five-week swing taking in Boston, Atlanta, Houston, Dallas, Fort Worth, Los Angeles, Denver and New York. In Denver I learned something very interesting from one of the brokers we visited. At the turn of the twentieth century his grandfather handled the insurances for the only two automobiles in the whole of the State of Colorado. Although they were located two to three hundred miles apart, they managed to collide with each other in downtown Denver! This crash wrecked the early Colorado Automobile Insurance statistics for many years. We finished in New York, returning home by sea on the *Queen Mary*. After that almost all my trips were done on my own initiative, subject to board approval.

They became more frequent as a result of a visit to London by Pete Glossop, a senior vice-president from Marsh & McLennan's Detroit office, when he paid a courtesy call on Ian Skimming. Ian was unavailable, and his secretary suggested that Pete should chat to me. We discussed details of the Casualty insurance requirements (Third Party Liability) for a utility known as American Natural Gas headquartered in Detroit. As I was now getting quite confident, I told him we could handle it (even though my main background at that time was Property as opposed to Casualty and the ANG offerings were purely Casualty). After Pete left the office, I gave the details to Keith Batchelor who seized upon them with delight and placed the risk within the next two days.

When Pete returned home he wrote to Ian, suggesting a visit by me to Marsh & McLennan's Detroit office. This was the start of many visits to that city where I became involved in successful acquisitions for Bowrings of large American accounts, primarily on a 'package basis' and mainly through the intervention of a senior vice-president of that office who had heard of the success of Marsh's Marine-based packages placed in London by Bowrings. The basic principles of a Non-Marine package were the same as a Marine-based package. My first was in respect of Chrysler and it worked as follows: we placed a $100 million policy anyone occurrence, sitting above, and/or in between, domestic policies: Excess Umbrella Liabilities above domestic primaries and self-insured retentions; Difference in Conditions between standard fire policies and 'All Risks'; 'Inland Marine' coverages in respect of all transit exposures, and so on.

During this visit I was privileged to be driven in the Chrysler experimental gas turbine car. I was told that fifty were made and leased to various persons in the United States for evaluation. Unfortunately, after the evaluations the cars had to be destroyed. Such a shame, as it was a very beautiful car. The reason, I was told, was that the bodies were imported from Italy under a special Customs agreement, the details of which I never fully understood.

I also witnessed some of the early experiments with car air bags as an alternative to seat belts.

Chrysler was followed by similar policies for a wide range of manufacturers. Pharmaceuticals or drug-related risks were beginning to become sensitive at this time. During my negotiations in the market for a very respectable pharmaceutical risk headquartered in Kalamazoo, I approached an important leading Marine underwriter in an attempt to persuade him to contribute to my placing in his Incidental Non-Marine account. He was another true gentleman of Lloyd's, Toby Green. His office outside Lloyd's comprised a couple of nondescript rooms above a shop in Leadenhall Market. I am sure he would not have had the least interest in working in more plush surroundings. He studied my slip with great care. After considering it for some time he said, most graciously, 'Graham, pharmaceuticals and drugs scare me. I'm sure if I take some of this stuff I'll finish up with trees growing out of my arse. Thank you for taking the trouble to come and see me.' Nevertheless, this risk was successfully completed without Toby's assistance and, in fact, was slightly 'overdone' so that all the lines subscribed had to be 'signed down'.

Incidental to the visit to the pharmaceutical company. I was able to sort out a misunderstanding regarding an insurance which had been taken out by the local Chamber of Commerce to pay in the event that the Kalamazoo Air Show had to be cancelled, which due to bad weather was what happened. The risk had been placed in the wrong market – Aviation – when it should have been placed in the Contingency market. As there hadn't been a crash or similar aviation loss, the Aviation underwriter had declined to pay. Fortunately, this problem was rapidly resolved to the satisfaction of all including the Aviation people who had originally 'misplaced' the risk.

While on a visit to Detroit, I called upon Seagrams, the whisky distillers, a Marsh & McLennan client, at their plant across the Detroit River in Windsor, Ontario. This was immediately followed by a journey to their plant in Peoria, Illinois, flying from Detroit via Chicago with the Seagrams Insurance Manager and the M&M vice-president in charge of the account. The flight to Chicago was on an ageing propeller DC6B. I sat with the Seagrams insurance manager. The M&M vice-president took an empty seat a couple of rows ahead of us. Just before departure he was joined by a professorial-looking gentleman and they were soon engaged in animated conversation. I was told later that the gentleman was a scientific boffin in the automobile industry and they had covered all kinds of subjects, each of which the 'professor' had shot down. Finally, the M&M vice-president in desperation had said, 'Well, at least there is one thing I think we can agree about, and that is how delightful the ladies are.' Unfortunately for him, the acoustics changed, as was common with those types of aircraft. There was a kind of silence or lull for a second or two during which all the passengers heard the 'professor' reply, 'Oh! So you like to screw, huh?'

Returning from Peoria to Chicago, where we had to change planes for Detroit, we found ourselves on the inaugural DC9 jet flight of a small local airline. Although it was midsummer, the weather was somewhat inclement and the plane was bouncing about. We had little pull-out plastic trays and had all been served drinks. Suddenly, I sensed we were in for a big bump and managed to save my drink from sliding off the tray. The other passengers, mostly businessmen in light summer suits, were not so lucky and their drinks landed in their laps. So coming off the flight at the gate in Chicago were two or three dozen businessmen who looked as though they had wet their pants – and, of course, in a way they had! A note, which a lot of passengers signed, had been passed to the captain, the message being that he should go back to pilot school. I thought this was most unfair as the flying conditions were extremely rough. That day's travels could not be described as ideal but I am glad to say the visit resulted in the successful placing of a package policy for Seagrams.

It was in Detroit, the centre of the American automobile industry, that the chairman of one of the largest automobile companies tried an experiment at one of his board meetings. When his fellow directors arrived, they found there was just a single chair available – reserved for the company secretary. Everyone else, including the chairman, had to stand. All the items on the agenda were satisfactorily discussed in a fraction of the time usually expended at such meetings.

For the geographer it is interesting to note that Detroit looks south into Canada. Apart from its industry, Detroit is a surprisingly interesting place to visit. It has superb suburbs, such as Grosse Pointe where there are some magnificent homes. Also there are several interesting museums, including most importantly the Henry Ford Museum and Greenfield Village. This complex is basically in two parts – first, the Henry Ford Museum building, covering about twelve acres and housing historical items of American life, including the contents of typical homes, steam transportation such as a huge transcontinental railroad engine, and a collection of nearly two hundred vehicles with many historical cars, including the presidential limousine in which President Kennedy was assassinated. The second part, Greenfield Village, is an open-air collection of buildings. Among the many fascinating exhibits are the Wright Brothers' Cycle Shop where they built their first airplane; the house of Noah Webster, of dictionary fame; and Thomas Edison's laboratory.

I accompanied one of my company's senior directors, Ronnie Cottle, in January 1966 on a visit to Montreal, our purpose being twofold – first, the financial and insurance requirements for the Churchill Falls Hydro-electric Scheme in Newfoundland; and, secondly, to take care of the insurance arrangements for the

Montreal Expo '67.

There were meetings with financiers and others regarding the proposed Churchill Falls Scheme which was under the auspices of the British Newfoundland Corporation (BRINCO). BRINCO's objectives were to further the interests of New-foundland with various projects. Bowrings had a financial interest and was a driving force in this organisation. The Churchill Falls project at that time was the biggest hydro-electric scheme to be proposed anywhere outside the USSR. This was very informative and we learned the basic details of the financial and construction proposals during these meetings. Amongst the various insurances the financiers were interested in obtaining was 'overrun' insur-ance, to pay in the event that the scheme was not completed by the scheduled date and/or cost a great deal more to complete than was envisaged. (Of all the great construction schemes since World War II, how many have been completed on time and within their original budgets? Consider the Channel Tunnel!).

The discussions were very complex. The idea was that the major customer would be the utility which supplied electricity to the City of New York and its surroundings. The obvious route for the transmission lines would be straight across the Province of Quebec in Canada. Although I sat in on these discussions, I was not involved personally with the arrangements for BRINCO to sell electricity to the Province of Quebec who, in turn, would sell it to the American utility on the southern border of the province. At first it was difficult to get agreement on suitable pricing, and it reached the point where serious suggestions were made that the Province of Quebec might be bypassed using an offshore cable. This would have been a very expensive way of sidestepping the then 'political' complications and would undoubtedly have created further insurance problems. Eventually, as usual, all was resolved, construction was authorised, and a colleague of mine dealt with the necessary insurance placings for this impressive scheme most successfully.

Concurrently with the Churchill Falls discussions, I was in-volved with the insurance programme for Montreal's Expo '67, a huge international trade fair organised by Quebec which was to be located mainly on an island in the St Lawrence River. The Expo authorities decided to have a Master Insurance Policy under the umbrella of which all exhibitors would buy their insurances. This policy turned out to be almost loss-free, but an interesting aside is that the one exhibitor who declined the insurance offered was a communist country whose exhibit incurred the only serious loss during the period of the exposition.

Consternation was caused to many citizens of Montreal who were living in high-rise apartments overlooking the Expo '67 site, when they observed in the early evening a 'monster' crossing the St Lawrence River and the shoreline ice, then proceeding through a car park and disappearing. Many phone calls were made to the police. The mysterious monster turned out to be an early hovercraft being tested for its possible use at the Expo site. This was the first appearance of that versatile vehicle in Canada.

There was an unforeseen interlude when a sudden unpredicted snowstorm hit the east of North America closing down all airports to the east of Chicago except one – Montreal. This necessitated many aircraft flying from the West Coast to eastern airports, as well as those on their way across the Atlantic, being diverted to Montreal where the French Canadian authorities at Dorval International Airport, together with air traffic controllers, did a superb job in receiving such an unprecedented number of aircraft in only a few hours. They kept the runways and taxi ways clear and managed to park the planes safely inside and outside the airport boundaries, even using the freeways. It was an astonishing sight.

A typical swing of five weeks' duration might take in eleven or twelve cities spanning the North American continent from north to south and east to west and could be enlivened by possible 'diversions'.

One Easter weekend, travelling from California to Chicago, I enjoyed a luxury train ride through the Rockies from Los Angeles to Willams where a bus took me to the South Rim of the Grand Canyon. Astride a mule I experienced the splendour of this natural wonder, riding from the rim down to the Colorado River where I stayed overnight, and riding back up to the rim the next day. At that time of year one went in a few hours from high to low desert, with small snowdrifts remaining at the top and very high temperatures at the bottom by the river.

On another occasion, I rented a car and drove from San Francisco to Los Angeles along the coast road, taking US Highway One through Monterey and Pebble Beach, stopping off for a tour of Hearst Castle – an impossibly splendid conglomeration of a magnificent residence and unusual taste with contemporary items, antiques and antiquities from anywhere in the world all mixed up, not forgetting a tomato ketchup bottle on a table elegantly laid for dinner. It really represented a large slice of history.

In the glory days of the transatlantic liners the normal method of transport for the swings would be to fly out, fly from city to city, and return to England from New York on either the *Queen Mary* or the *Queen Elizabeth*. Invariably, one would bump into a friendly competitor or an underwriter on the ship. Those sea trips were a great way of unwinding, with time to compile notes and prepare reports on the business undertaken, and there were many interesting episodes for the observant passenger on the voyage home.

One passenger attempted to get into the *Guinness Book of Records* by 'swimming across the Atlantic'. We visited him regularly at the first-class pool where he solemnly made his way back and forth, being fed and watered (and ginned!) at suitable intervals. He left the pool only for essential toiletry activities.

At a crowded bar a lady had a bright red cocktail accidentally spilt over her pure white evening dress. Within seconds the bartender seized a soda siphon and to her astonished horror, as well as that of the bystanders, squirted the contents on to the stain, which covered most of her bosom. He instructed her to go immediately to her stateroom stewardess who would take care of things. The next evening the lady was again wearing her white dress which was immaculate. Soda really does work if applied promptly!

Early one evening I was in the splendid bar which overlooked the ship's bows and witnessed one of my fellow passengers, the late Herbert Morrison, having an altercation with the head bartender. Morrison wanted to take a large corner of the bar space for a private party. It was explained, most politely, that the bar itself could not be reserved, nor any part of it, but he was welcome to take a private room adjacent to the bar. Morrison surprisingly retorted to the well-mannered bartender, 'Do you know who I am?'

'Yes, sir, you used to be a member of the Cabinet. But you cannot book space in this bar – no one can'.

Not all was plain sailing. On one occasion an enormous wave swept over the ship. The view from the forward bar was an astounding sight as we appeared to be going straight into a cliff. There was quite a lot of damage and some passengers suffered minor injuries. Another time a big wave hit the ship while after dinner dancing was in progress. Most of us finished up on one side of the ballroom floor in a long heap on top of each other, togged up of course in our evening finery, with everybody laughing like hell... and the band played on.

Once, things got a bit difficult on arrival in England. A senior director of mine used to take parties of friends on safari in Africa. Just before I left for one of my swings, he asked me to bring him back a supply of insect repellent of a type which was only obtainable in North America. Because it was the wrong season I had been unsuccessful in buying any until the very day I was due to sail from New York, when I found a drugstore which sold me all its remaining stock – twelve bottles and twelve sticks. Fine. I felt very pleased and self-satisfied until I declared this purchase to Customs at Southampton. It was about three o'clock in the afternoon. I was taken to a back room where all the insect repellents were analysed. My person and my luggage were closely examined, and it wasn't until nine o'clock in the evening that I was cleared and permitted to leave with all my possessions and purchases. The director was so pleased that I had successfully accomplished my mission on his behalf! Upon reflection, I realised it must have looked very suspicious returning to England carrying twenty-four tropical insect repellents on behalf of another person.

After my fifth return trip by courtesy of Cunard on one or other of the *Queens*, this wonderful method of travel ceased. Flying was faster. Sadly, air travel supplanted the great era of transatlantic crossings by sea.

Typical swings during my time with Bowrings would be: Los

Angeles – San Francisco – Portland – Seattle – Vancouver – Minneapolis-St Paul – Kansas City – St Louis – Philadelphia – New York; or Chicago – Milwaukee – Detroit – Toronto – Montreal – Washington – Boston – Philadelphia; or Detroit – Cleveland – Pittsburgh – Nashville – Memphis – Atlanta – Savannah – Tallahassee – Fort Lauderdale – Miami – Puerto Rico. There were many other variations. I was most fortunate to be able to see most of North America on an expense account with first-class travel. With such involved itineraries, there is absolutely no doubt I could not have carried out these trips competently had I been flying economy class!

The local newspapers kept us up to date with what was going on in each of the places visited. During one of the swings, my wife rang down to the hotel desk to order room service for breakfast, and asked for a Cleveland newspaper.

The receptionist was surprised.

'I'm afraid that's going to be a little difficult. Would you like one of our papers?'

'Why,' asked my wife, 'Where are we?'

'Minneapolis, ma 'am.'

'Oh my God, Cleveland was yesterday!'

My wife regaled her with our seven-cities-in-three-weeks itinerary.

The receptionist laughed, 'Sounds like that movie – If it's Tuesday, this must be Belgium'.

Chicago was a frequent call on many of my swings, and on one of these I was there when the John Hancock Building was in its very early stages of construction on Michigan Avenue. Anyone familiar with the sight of this splendid building will appreciate that it looks by its very shape as if it is standing on four feet, similar in some ways to the Eiffel Tower or Blackpool Tower, but clad like a normal office block. This is how it appeared to me when I first saw it, consisting of steelwork rising some forty feet out of the ground from its four corners. There was a problem with the foundations at one of the corners, and an American company with a 25 per cent line on the Construction Risk insurance had opted out or exercised its right to cancel. I was asked whether I had a market to replace this 25 per cent. A couple of phone calls to London and the 25 per cent had been replaced in the Lloyd's market as new business. This was a classic example of a combination of servicing existing accounts and obtaining an interesting piece of new business at the same time.

On that trip I became involved with turkeys. The main problem here is that these birds are basically stupid. Turkey farmers in the Midwest, where the weather can get very cold, provide heated accommodation for their birds. When icy winds blow down from Canada, instead of getting into the warm accommodation provided, some turkeys tend to huddle together outside so that the ones in the middle of the huddle suffocate and those on the outside freeze to death. There is another problem with them. Should a turkey which is walking determinedly east or west meet another turkey walking equally determinedly north or south, the one made to stop will get so frustrated and angry that it can have a seizure and die. In spite of all these idiosyncrasies, we were able to provide a satisfactory insurance programme for the turkey farmers.

Fish farming in the Southern States is big business. The type of fish being bred have a tendency to climb out of their ponds and walk off, taking up residence in other ponds. It was very difficult to devise a reasonable kind of insurance against such activities, but one of my colleagues succeeded.

Mortality insurance on animals is a complex and expensive business. To insure each individual animal in a zoo against risks of mortality would be prohibitive. We therefore devised a policy for zoo owners which worked like this. The zoo owner would have to provide us with detailed information for the preceding five to ten years of their 'dying costs' by species. We then approached underwriters to obtain coverage excess of, say, 110 per cent, 115 per cent, or whatever per cent of their average annual expenses for the replacement of their animals. This was in some ways an adaptation of the Carpenter Plan or Burning Cost type of coverage. It provided chronological stabilisation for the finances of a zoo and could be said to resemble a variation of Abnormal Mortality Reinsurance which some Life Assurance companies buy. This scheme was taken up by a number of zoos in the United States. This principle of chronological stabilisation which my colleagues and I dreamed up for the finances of a zoo is easily adaptable to many other businesses – for example, Physical Damage on a fleet of buses or trucks or a large airline fleet, or on a retail operation with many outlets, and similar businesses where the physical assets are not concentrated in one area. A number of such policies were placed but were not popular with brokers or insurance companies if only because they reduced the brokerage for the brokers and investment income for the insurance companies.

A peril against which it is very difficult to be prepared in advance is fraud. Before banks became involved in electronic data processing and computers, they used to have on their customers' tables in the banking halls slots containing blank paying-in slips. Those readers who are old enough will recall that if they wished to pay money into their bank they would take one of these slips, fill in the details and hand the slip together with the cash/cheques to the cashier. The transaction was thus safely completed. When the banks changed to chequebooks with customised paying-in slips which included pre-printed details of the individual's account, it was regarded as a huge advance in the process of banking. This changeover resulted in what can only be described as a brilliant one-off fraud. In an American city, a clever individual removed all the paying-in slips from his new chequebook and put them in the slots which used to contain the bank's own blank paying-in slips. Many people fell for the bait, using the fraudster's paying-in slips which they had picked up from where the bank's normal supply of blanks used to be available, with the result that all these individuals' cheques and cash were credited to the fraudster's account.

Another clever scam involved a bank which had twenty cashiers positions. A customer visited the bank manager and paid in a cheque for $50,000, explaining that one day next week he would be concluding a deal and it would be necessary for him to impress the other party by sending one of his clerks to the bank to cash a cheque for $50,000 – and he did not want any delays or queries. The bank manager instructed all his cashiers that somebody from the XYZ Company would be cashing a cheque next week for $50,000 which must not be queried. Sure enough, the next week a cheque was duly presented to one of the cashiers for $50,000 upon which payment was made. At precisely the same time, identical cheques were being presented for encashment at the other nineteen cashiers' positions.

A very much larger fraud involved bank loans granted on warehouse receipts, which became known as the 'Great Salad Oil Swindle'. In this case, a Chicago bank had been advancing money on such receipts until one of their executives doing a random check suddenly realised that some warehouse receipts, from one source only, represented more than the entire world's production of salad oil. It is a complicated story, but it was quite simple in its operation. The capacity of an oil tank was normally tested by the use of a dipstick inserted through a small covered aperture in the top of the tank. Inside the tank, immediately below the aperture, had been welded a tube the volume of which took up a very small proportion of the tank's capacity. The dipstick used by the examiners or inspectors would thereby show the tank to be full, whereas the tank was in fact empty except for the contents of this small tube.

Another dipstick story concerned a whisky distillery where, despite strict security, a nightwatchman would emerge from his post each morning quite drunk. It was discovered that while on duty he spent some of his time sliding a square shaped dipstick into and out of a vat and laboriously wiping the whisky off the sides of the dipstick into his coffee mug.

There is no limit to the ingenuity which may be developed by determined fraudsters. In the days when almost all transactions in retail outlets involved the transfer of cash, shops, restaurants, garages, pubs, etc., used bank night safes for the secure overnight safety of their takings. Some night safes would accumulate substantial amounts of untraceable cash. A clever thief constructed a strong-looking steel box complete with the bank's logo prominently displayed, a letterbox-type slit with an inward working flap, and a notice stating that the night safe was 'Out of Order' and to 'Please Use This Temporary Arrangement'. It was securely chained to the decorative railings outside the bank and quite a number of innocent traders fell for this ruse. Of course, the imitation night safe and its deposits had disappeared by the time the bank opened next morning.

There are many variations of policy forms which give coverage against financial and other fraudulent activities, and can even be extensions of other standard policies. A banker's blanket bond is just one example.

Now for something quite different. In 1957 the successful injection into an earth orbit of the Russian 'Sputnik', which was about the size of an orange, fired off an entirely new industry and method of telecommunications which did not require unreliable land lines or radio communications ridden with static.

This sparked a major step forward for radio, television, and telephones, not to mention attendant military possibilities. The first serious commercial application of this new advance was developed by the American corporation COMSAT (Communications Satellite Corporation), which devised a system for putting sophisticated satellites into orbit around the world, to which and from which radio communications could be transmitted directly (i.e., line of sight). Insurance was needed, and Lloyd's was the obvious place to explore the possibilities. We set up a meeting in one of the conference rooms and amongst those present were representatives from Bowrings, COMSAT, the American producing broker, and numerous underwriters from all markets – Aviation, Marine, Non-Marine, etc. This meeting was very instructive. The requirement was that the satellite be placed in orbit around the world in a stationary position relative to the earth. Imagine that the hub of a bicycle wheel is the earth and the valve on the tyre is the satellite. The valve is always in the same position relative to the hub. This was the equivalent of putting a six-ft block or sphere through a seven-ft square window three or four hundred miles away. Should the satellite not have arrived in its correct orbit when it went through the 'window', the line of sight would 'creep' so that for many hours out of twenty-four it would be useless for its intended purpose. The insurance required was to pay in the event that the satellite did not arrive in its proper orbit in relation to the earth.

The only real help we could get was that COMSAT would be using an obsolescent military rocket, known as a Delta 3-Stage Long-Tank, which had been tested in firings down into the South

Atlantic. The information we were permitted to have was limited about these tests but very useful and helpful for underwriters in assessing the risk. COMSAT intended to place five satellites into correct orbits at a cost of $5 million each. This figure covered transportation of each satellite from its place of manufacture to its lift-off point and thence into its proper orbit. After much deliberation, and questions and answers, underwriters came up with what could only have been in those days a typical Lloyd's inspired but profitable speculative guess – a premium of $1 million per shot, with the proviso that they only paid for four out of five failures. All five shots were successful.

COMSAT developed into INTELSAT, and the business of communication satellites grew rapidly to the point where a very expensive satellite was recovered after its launch had gone wrong, the recovery expenses of which were paid by Lloyd's – and here we are talking of a figure around $100 million. Once again, Lloyd's played a major part in the commercial development of advanced technology.

Early in my insurance career at Bowrings, I was on the fringes of a committee consisting of representatives from broking companies and underwriting organisations which looked into the problems pertaining to nuclear facilities insurances. From the deliberations of this committee the Nuclear Incident Exclusion Clauses were devised. The intention was to make insurance available for such things as nuclear power stations, radioactive isotopes, tracers, and other investigative activities in medicine and industry generally. These deliberations resulted in the formation of NEPIA and NELIA, the Nuclear Insurance Pools for Physical Damage and Third Party Liability, respectively. The committee was addressed by various experts in the field of nuclear energy. During one of the meetings I asked the scientists what would happen if something should go wrong. I used the expression 'run wild', and was treated like a naughty schoolboy who had uttered a rude word in class. 'It simply couldn't happen,' they said. This, of course, was well before the Three Mile Island and Windscale disasters and a very long time before Chernobyl.

It confirmed my opinion that the proper definition of an 'expert' is where X is the unknown factor and spurt is a drip under pressure, and this always comes to mind whenever I hear that an expert is about to proclaim on any subject. It makes me blush when I think of the time I gave evidence in a California court about insurance matters and was myself described as an 'expert witness'!

An interesting risk in which I was involved – not in its placing but in the loss settlement – was the Moscow Olympics in 1980. The broker who had placed this several years before the event had left my company's employment. The risk was twofold: cancellation of the event, or 'no show' by the American team. The insured was an American television company who were investing large sums of money to ensure that their coverage of the Olympics would be first class, as their revenues for so doing would be coming from advertisers. No American company or corporation would be likely to advertise during this television coverage if the American team was not participating. The Moscow Olympics were not cancelled, but there was 'no show' by the American *team* because relations between the two countries were not at their best. Two or three American athletes did turn up for the Games, but not as an American team. This gave an opportunity for some underwriters on the policy to suggest that there had been a 'show' by an 'American team'. It took me a weekend of studying the original placing files from three or four years previously to produce a few sentences which persuaded underwriters to pay the loss – which was very substantial.

Insurance provides businesses and individual citizens protection of all kinds against the many ordinary and extraordinary perils which may beset them:

- Multiple Births insurance, previously known as Twin insurance, is now almost unobtainable because of the availability of fertility drugs, but it did serve a need for many years at a reasonable price.

- Film Producers' Indemnity insurances were developed at Lloyd's after World War II. The cover was very broad and protected the producers' investments in the production of a given film. For example, the shooting may be almost complete and one of the stars might die, or drop out because of serious illness. In such a case all monies expended up until that time would have been wasted. Such sums were recoverable under a film producers' indemnity policy which could be extended to cover the reasonably estimated box office receipts from the completed film.

- During one of the early 1950s general elections, the Liberal Party fielded candidates for almost every seat in the House of Commons. They took the precaution of insuring all their candidates' deposits which are required to be put up for any person standing as a Member of Parliament. This insurance could in no way have been described as profitable for the underwriters who had provided the coverage!

- Directors' and Officers' Liability insurance is now a must for all businesses. This covers the directors and officers of corporations against suits brought by stockholders or members of the public who feel aggrieved about actions taken by directors and officers and the corporations which they serve. These can range from such things as financial mismanagement of various kinds, bad or misjudged acquisitions of other companies, to insufficient insurance protecting the activities of the business. There are many other examples which the reader will not have difficulty in envisaging because in this increasingly litigious world suits can be brought so easily.

- Kidnap and Ransom insurance had been available at Lloyd's since the 1930s, but it really developed from about the 1960s onwards.

- Police Officers' Professional Liability, which is closely coupled with the liability of law enforcement agencies or police departments, protects such individuals or organisations against suits by members of the public. Suits could involve actions for wrongful arrest, the infringement of civil rights, or simply the failure of the police to carry out their duties. Policies were extended to cover police officers killed or injured on or off duty during their service. I negotiated such policies on behalf of police departments in

Florida, Georgia, and elsewhere.

- Just before ground clearance was undertaken for the 1965 Bowring Building on Tower Hill, Ian Skimming obtained a Lloyd's policy to pay in the event that a discovery of archaeological importance necessitated a 'dig' delaying the completion date expected at Bowrings, their architects and contractors. There was no claim on the policy, but such policies have been of inestimable value to many since that time.

Everybody talks about the weather – a safe subject for opening a conversation. But the weather can also have frightening and expensive consequences – an important factor in the insurance business. Some readers may have seen the extraordinary newsreels of the destruction in 1940 of the Tacoma Narrows Bridge in the State of Washington. Being of the suspension type, the bridge was whipped into snakelike convolutions until it collapsed. Following such a splendid display of acrobatics the bridge was named, most appropriately, 'Galloping Gertie'. I was reminded of this when the Millennium Bridge over the River Thames had to be closed because of a fit of the wobbles. Galloping Gertie's problem was caused by wind currents. This was an example of a loss occurring, the cause of which had not been properly anticipated. Disturbances in the atmosphere very broadly referred to as wind can have many manifestations. Wind, which is air moving rapidly from one area to another, can have speeds ranging from a few miles per hour to in excess of one hundred miles per hour. Wind, in its various forms has cost insurers dearly throughout the world.

A tornado is a windstorm with very special characteristics. It is quite simply an enlarged version of a little whirlwind which may cross one's garden, throwing the leaves around in a tight ascending circle, very rarely more than one yard across, arising and disappearing for no apparent reason. This is an embryonic tornado. A full-blown one can be really vicious. I had a frightening experience in Indiana when during lunch in a restaurant the owner announced there was a tornado warning. Early American settlers dug their own personal tornado shelters and pulled the lid down over them until the storm had passed. We all had to go down to the safety of the basement and were able to observe everything from the street-level windows. We were on the periphery of the tornado. There was what resembled a dark grey or black stick, maybe a quarter of a mile wide, rotating within itself very rapidly and travelling somewhat haphazardly, destroying or sucking up everything in its path. This was accompanied by a fierce hailstorm on the edge of the tornado itself, which was so violent that the hailstones stripped the paint off parked automobiles. My immediate reaction was, 'Look at those cars – they're suddenly silver!' The tornado left a swathe of destruction with no obvious pattern, just a winding track through a built-up area which looked as though it had been bombed. After the excitement was over, everyone in the restaurant went back upstairs and continued with lunch. That tornado was formed on land, but they can also start at sea and produce equally frightening waterspouts.

Hurricanes are normally spawned at sea and seem to reach their greatest violence on crossing a coastal strip. Once a wind exceeds 75 miles per hour it is generally referred to as a hurricane. It can be very wide ranging in its travels, covering large areas at the same time. Geographically, hurricane territory encompasses the Gulf of Mexico and islands in the Caribbean and the Bahamas. The hurricane season usually starts at about the end of July and finishes at the end of September. American states which may expect to be visited are mainly Texas, Louisiana, Florida, Georgia, and South and North Carolina. States north of the Carolinas are rarely affected. There are hurricane areas starting in the Pacific to the west of Mexico, and, of course, typhoons in the Pacific and Indian Oceans from Indonesia north to Japan. One of the most notable hurricanes as far as the United States is concerned was 'Betsy' in 1965, which devastated many of the South-Eastern States. The insured loss of 'Betsy' was in excess of $600 million. If that 1965 figure was translated into the real equivalent of figures for the year 2000, it would by today's standards be truly horrendous.

Flooding can be a frightening hazard. Kansas City is a transportation centre which grew up as a major crossing of the Missouri River in pioneer days. It is interesting in that it straddles two States – Kansas and Missouri – so there are two Kansas Cities, one in each state. Bowrings had produced a sizeable and varied amount of insurance business from this area, including trucking and transportation generally together with Difference in Conditions insurances which provided coverage for the difference between standard local policies and 'All Risks'. Also, because of its location well and truly in the Midwest, there was a substantial amount of livestock business. A flash flood hit the area a couple of days before my wife and I arrived there on one of my visits. Heavy rainstorms had caused water to sweep through the downtown areas taking with it all in its path. A natural watercourse, usually dry, running through these areas had been concreted some years previously. Consequently, the extra water could not seep away and shops and restaurants were inundated to a height of about five feet. By the time we arrived the water had receded, leaving in its wake a tidemark on the buildings. Cars were lying at all angles having been swept across tennis courts and parking lots, clearly visible from the hotel. There was emergency lighting in our room. The underground garage was still flooded, and the hotel management were apprehensive about what they might eventually find. While I was visiting insurance brokers my wife visited the shopping centre. Everywhere was open for business. A large department store, with a muddy line on the walls of the ground floor level, had huge fans drying out the premises. Further along the street shopkeepers had put furniture out on the sidewalks in the warmth of the sunshine while the staff cleared up the mess inside. The local people were coping with the aftermath of the flood philosophically and with exceptionally good humour.

The four elements, earth, air, fire and water, were supposed by the ancients to be the foundation of all things – except in China where wood was the fifth element. These elements all feature prominently in insurance.

I was asked whether we could place insurances on valuable homes located in the brush fire area above the city of Los Angeles. This area has beautiful views down the hills across to the city and the Pacific Ocean, but it is very hazardous as a fire risk. I was taken by a broker up into the district to learn a little about it. The

111

day was very hot, over 100° Fahrenheit. The oppressive dry heat gave a sense of uneasiness, especially on the dirt roads which we had taken as a short cut of some thirty miles and which were just wide enough for the car to get through the tinder-like brush. This was emphasised when we had a puncture. While we were changing the wheel, I could not help developing a sense of foreboding and helplessness in the silence which was broken only by the snapping sounds of overheated brushwood. We continued our journey, and on our way to the relative safety of the inhabited areas were stopped by a police car and warned there was a high fire risk alert.

After many miles, we reached some lovely homes where most of the owners had taken the proper precautions to safeguard them by removing the brush from their properties. Large sections had also been removed from the immediate vicinity of each local community. My broker friend cut a small piece of brushwood which he put in the boot of his car. We returned to his home which had a tiled patio where he dropped the brushwood and invited me to put a match to it to see what would happen. The brushwood exploded as if it was soaked in high-octane fuel. With the information available and insistence upon suitable precautions, cover for such properties was arranged at Lloyd's.

On another visit to California, this time in the San Francisco area, my wife and I were shown examples of people's stupidity in planting eucalyptus trees close to their homes, in one case building a house around one of these trees as the central feature. Eucalyptus is not native to California, having been imported from Australia, and its flammable properties are almost as dangerous as the brushwood in Southern California.

Sometimes meetings with clients could result in most unusual and interesting consequences. In the summer of 1984 the City Fathers of the Salt Lake City Corporation, a client of Marsh & McLennan, wanted to know how the City of London refurbished or modernised its historic old buildings. At that time I was a Common Councilman of the Corporation of London – the local government of the City of London – and thus able to arrange for Phil Erickson of the office of the mayor of Salt Lake City to visit the City of London's planning department at Guildhall. My wife and I found that we shared with Phil an interest in horticulture. We told him of our fascination with the Giant Saguaro cacti. At dusk they seemed to be walking about and talking to each other in the Arizona Desert. He said he would be delighted to arrange for one of these extraordinary plants to be sent from Salt Lake City Corporation as a gift to the City of London and be placed in the Barbican Conservatory in the City of London. Little did we know – the Giant Saguaro being a protected species – that it would take a year to resolve the red tape on both sides of the Atlantic. In August 1985, Salt Lake City confirmed that the relevant papers had been released, but before packing the cactus for transportation, my wife and I were invited as guests of Mayor Palmer De Paulis and the Corporation of Salt Lake City to accept it personally on behalf of the Corporation of London.

Included in a swing between Seattle and New York was a week in Salt Lake City when we were lavishly entertained, introduced to many interesting people, invited to lunch by the Elders of the Mormon Church, attended the Sunday morning broadcast by the Mormon Tabernacle Choir, shown the site of the new arboretum under construction, made honorary police officers of the Salt Lake City Police Department, and taken by air taxi to Lake Powell (some call it a 'Grand Canyon with water') where we visited the Glen Canyon Dam and travelled by boat to see Rainbow Bridge, carved out of red rock by water and wind and a sacred site for the Navajo.

A meeting was arranged with Lorraine Miller of Cactus Growers of Utah. Lined up for inspection in her desert plant greenhouse were three cacti which had been sent wrapped in carpeting from her suppliers in California, who had obtained them under licence from Arizona. We chose the fattest, 3 ft high and weighing about 150 lbs, and named it 'Fred'. The problem was getting 'Fred' to London. No less than three states authorities – Arizona, California, and Utah – together with the federal authority in Virginia – were involved in arranging export licences. David Jones, superintendent of the City of London Parks and Gardens Department, successfully dealt with the British authorities, who had to be satisfied that all these licenses were in order before they would allow the cactus through immigration at

Heathrow.

In March 1986 'Fred', wrapped in polythene, was put into a 5 ft x 2 ft casket and flown to Los Angeles where it joined a direct flight to Heathrow, arriving on Good Friday and being collected by David Jones after the Easter holiday. Insurance had been arranged through Lloyd's for the complicated transportation arrangements from the United States to England on behalf of this rare and valuable specimen. Because the import of soil is not allowed it all had to be removed from the plant's roots before packing, so the cactus was carefully potted up at the City of London's nurseries at West Ham Park before being installed in the Barbican Conservatory. 'Fred' became something of a celebrity and in May was taken along to meet the Queen Mother at Sadlers Hall where she was attending a Sheriff's luncheon.

On one of my visits to Canada in the spring, a broker friend took me to his summer home which he was opening up after it had been closed for the winter. This was a nice log cabin, the only residence on an island in a lake about two hundred miles north of Montreal. A local ferryman delivered us and waited while we checked that everything was all right. This was just as well, as we discovered that during the winter the cabin had been visited by bears walking to it across the ice and forcing their way through the door. It was 'Goldilocks' in reverse. There were muddy paw prints all over the floors. The bears had had a lot of fun pulling the telephone off the wall, sitting on the chairs which were all smashed, and sleeping on the beds which were broken and in a complete mess; it was also obvious that these uninvited guests were not potty-trained. The icebox had been prised open but it was empty (presumably to their annoyance). Being clever animals, they will always discover the bear necessities, so had turned their attention to the kitchen cupboards, tucking into all the non-perishables... sugar, biscuits, jam, cornflakes, and packets of flour. My friend commented ruefully that when they had finished they must have looked more like polar bears. They had even investi-gated the boathouse. The boat, unable to support their weight, had sunk. With the help of the ferryman we tidied the place as best we could and went back to the mainland where we arranged for repair people to clean up the mess. Also, we weren't too sure if the bears had returned to the mainland for the summer or were lurking in the woods close by observing us from the safety of the trees. There was nothing else to do but return to Montreal – an aborted and b-ruined weekend! That was another type of insured loss by Lloyd's that was new to me – use and occupancy by bears.

Bowrings had several business producers in the delightful and historic city of Boston, the most notable being Boit, Dalton & Church, where Keith Batchelor worked for a couple of years or so. He assisted Colby Hewitt, one of Boit's executives, to set up a Surplus Lines operation known as Maritime Underwriters. This agency became a very good producer of both insurance and reinsurance business for Bowrings, and Keith's sojourn in Boston with Maritime Underwriters gave a tremendous boost to Bowrings in the enlargement of their direct North American Non-Marine business as opposed to reinsurance, particularly on his return to London. Boston became a regular port of call for the Bowring Non-Marine travellers on their swings. I happened to be there one year on 19 April – Patriots Day – and found that 19 April is a good excuse for a party, all the more so if the locals have in their possession a captive Englishman.

Patriots Day celebrates the episode in 1775 when Paul Revere signalled by lantern from the tower of the Old North Church that British troops had set off along the Concord Road. He then galloped from Boston to Lexington and Concord to warn John Adams and John Hancock so they could escape before the British arrived. I was told that we would witness the annual re-enactment of the ride from the Old North Church to Lexington and Concord, following the procession headed by a horseman taking the part of Paul Revere, after which there would be a magnificent party but I would not be allowed a drink unless I could recite at least the first eight lines of Longfellow's poem, 'The Landlord's Tale'. I went to a bookshop, obtained a copy of the poem and burned the midnight oil swotting up its one hundred and thirty lines. Came the day and the party. I started off, 'Listen, my children, and you shall hear/Of the midnight ride of Paul Revere,' and had progressed as far as 'One, if by land, and two, if by sea' when shouts of 'Enough!' came from the assembled company and I was well fêted. None of my American hosts could remember past the fifth line!

Being a Lloyd's man, I was fully cognisant of the fact that without insurance there could be no reinsurance. Conversely, reinsurance is a complementary part of insurance. Of course, a traveller to North America during my time was expected to be able to discuss both these subjects with reasonable confidence and understanding, except for those travelling on reinsurance treaty business who were highly specialised and would understand very little of the problems involved in the day-to-day workings of direct insurance. Some reinsurance brokers in North America were owned by insurance brokers. New York was very interesting in that certain individuals in the reinsurance business were touchy about those in the insurance business. They actually seemed to believe that insurance and reinsurance were two totally different subjects and had to be kept at arm's length from each other. This probably arose if one knows that insurance has been defined as the 'nuts and bolts' whereas reinsurance has been defined as the 'art of juggling figures'.

It was brought home to me unexpectedly when visiting a reinsurance broker one afternoon, having seen an insurance broker during that morning. My discussions were interrupted by a senior executive who told me it was inappropriate for me to visit insurance and reinsurance brokers during the same trip as it was, in his opinion, a conflict of interest. His behaviour was most unusual and not what the competent honest London broker expected in such a sophisticated insurance fraternity. In New York or Chicago or San Francisco, as in London, anybody who was anybody in the insurance or reinsurance business knew everybody else either personally or indirectly or by repute, who was in town, and who was visiting whom. So it was well known that I was representing Bowrings at many different offices in New York on both insurance and reinsurance business. That senior executive's attitude was totally inexplicable and I never experienced it in any other American city or on any other occasion. It was even more puzzling when one considers that a Lloyd's underwriter may look at many insurances and reinsurances during his working day. This was the first time that I heard that totally misunderstood, but useful to some, expression – conflict of interest. It is my belief that insurance and reinsurance are so intermingled that to be a good 'insurance man' one has to be competent in both spheres.

Of my many trips to New York three produced a curious and weird experience at Kennedy Airport. On the first occasion I arrived at the United Airlines terminal from Denver and took a cab downtown to Manhattan. The driver made a great point of telling me that he hadn't been to the airport for nearly six months because he hated going there and avoided it whenever possible. About three months later I arrived at the BOAC terminal from London. To my astonishment the waiting cab driver was the same one. He recognised me, and said he hadn't been back to the airport since he had picked me up from the United Airlines terminal. One would have thought that was a good enough story on its own, but about a year later I arrived at the Eastern Airlines terminal on a flight from Boston and, sure enough, the same cab driver was waiting for me. His opening comment was, 'Oh no – I can't take you.' But he did. The three terminals are a long way apart from each other, and on the way into New York City the cab driver and I tried to work out the odds against these triple coincidental meetings.

New York City has always been a wonderful place, whether for business or for pleasure. When I first became familiar with it the insurance and financial district was concentrated in the Wall Street area. I am told that as a certain new building was completed in the early 1930s it had a sub-basement designed to be a restaurant. This building was completed about the same time that Prohibition ended. It was also during the Depression, and no tenant could be found to take over the restaurant. The story goes that just across the street in a niche of another building was a mobile hot dog stand run by two brothers. In desperation, the owner of the newly constructed building offered the restaurant to these busy entrepreneurs. As an inducement they were told the only rent they would have to pay would be the price of the rolls and butter they sold. The brothers took it. This restaurant and bar became a very successful downtown financial New York watering hole, especially after some insurance brokers took over the upper floors of the building. The bartenders seemed to know all their customers, never measured out a drink, never appeared to take cash, and presented the regulars with their bills at the end of the week. During one of my visits I needed to cash a cheque at about three o'clock in the afternoon, and this busy bar which had been serving drinks, sandwiches and snacks since ten o'clock that morning could only scrape up $33 out of all the tills. Naturally, the place was very popular with the insurance fraternity. On one of my earlier trips to New York Vodka Martinis were all the fashion. The office head of one of the large insurance brokers told his staff he would prefer they went back to Gin Martinis so that their clients knew they were under the influence of alcohol and not just plain stupid!

The telephone number PA.6-5000 of the Statler Hotel (now the Statler Hilton) was made famous by Glenn Miller and his Orchestra when in residence there with the song 'Pennsylvania Six Five Thousand'. One time when I was staying at the Statler I left a phone message for a colleague who was booked in at another hotel in New York. His wife picked the message up from the desk. The Statler's number had been written out in full. She thought 'Pennsylvania Six Five Thousand' was a joke and the message was never passed on!

Washington DC is a most impressive city with its many focal points such as the Lincoln Memorial and the Washington Monument. The land was donated by the states of Maryland and Virginia. George Washington selected the exact spot for 'Federal City' and Thomas Jefferson was the first president to be inaugurated in Washington itself. Designed by a Frenchman, Pierre L'Enfant, and laid out by Andrew Ellicott, it has a gridiron arrangement of streets cut by diagonal avenues radiating from the Capitol and the White House. One of the insurance brokers I called upon during my visits happened to be connected with the party then in power and arranged for me to be given a one-to-one private guided tour of the White House. President Nixon was not in residence, and I was therefore able to see the Oval Room and most of its associated offices within this fascinating and historic building.

There were occasions on the swings when difficulties had to be overcome. A misfortune befell a friendly competitor of mine when we were both visiting Toronto. He had taken time off to visit Niagara Falls and while there decided to cross the bridge connecting Canada and the United States. Having left the Canadian side, he wandered along admiring the Falls from this truly spectacular viewpoint. Arriving on the American side, he was not allowed in as he had left his passport with his American visa back at the hotel in Canada. To his dismay the Canadian authorities wouldn't let him in either without his passport. It took a complicated arrangement with a taxi driver, telephones, and the cooperation of the management of his hotel for him to be reunited with his passport, and taught him not to take time off for fun in the middle of a business trip unless he had previously assessed the situation and taken all necessary precautions.

It is very easy for the traveller to put his foot in it by unwittingly upsetting national susceptibilities. This happened to me with Air Canada when I wanted to re-confirm a flight from Toronto to New York. There were two waiting areas, one designated 'International' and the other 'Domestic'. Naturally, I took my place in a long queue in the 'International' section only to be told when I eventually got to the desk that I should have joined the 'Domestic' queue. My remark that I wasn't aware Canada had become part of the United States went over like a lead balloon.

One of my swings was memorably fraught when my wife and I left on a BOAC flight for Detroit from Heathrow on a Saturday morning, having met a colleague and his wife who were departing about half an hour later for Bermuda, an important centre for 'offshore' insurance companies. On arrival in Detroit, friends took us to our hotel and called for us at seven o'clock in the evening (one o'clock Sunday morning London time) to take us out to dinner. We finally got back to our hotel at one o'clock in the morning Detroit time. We had left home at eight o'clock on Saturday morning and went to bed at seven o'clock the following morning London time – twenty-three hours on the go. We were woken at seven o'clock in the morning by a phone call from England telling us that my father had died. The next two hours or so were spent rearranging the flights between cities and visits to clients. We took the afternoon flight back to London with the same cabin crew from the previous day, who looked after us with great kindness and extra special care. On arrival at Heathrow, we learned from our Bowring chauffeur that my colleague and his wife had returned from Bermuda because they had had a similar bereavement. The itinerary of the swing had to be changed, starting in Denver the following Friday – which meant changing planes in Chicago. The flight from Chicago to Denver was brightened for us as Bob Hope was sitting across the aisle. The only Bowring clients who were inconvenienced by the rearrangements were those in Detroit and Chicago who were visited at the end of the trip instead of at the beginning of it. We had crossed the Atlantic three times in one week.

Aviation

Travelling on behalf of Lloyd's originally meant that if business was in Japan a person of my father's generation took a train to Southampton, a ship to New York, a train to the West Coast of the United States, and a ship to Tokyo. The return would be the reverse procedure unless a complicated journey could be arranged via the Trans-Siberian Railway. Such a round trip would take months. The aeroplane changed all that (some would say not necessarily for the better!).

Aviation as such started in the eighteenth century with the use of baskets hanging under hot air balloons. These were eventually adapted for military purposes and used for observation during the siege of Paris in the 1870s. In the archives of an American life insurance company in the early 1960s was found a policy dating back to the 1890s which had travelling by balloon specifically excluded.

Concurrent with the development of balloons, heavier-than-air machines progressed rapidly after the Wright Brothers' successful flight in 1903. And shortly after the crossing of the English Channel by Louis Blériot in 1909, various newspapers began offering prizes for successful flights from London to Manchester and elsewhere.

In early 1914 my mother, then a young girl, had a friend who was a lieutenant in the Air Arm of the Royal Engineers which became the Royal Flying Corps. He was doing his flying at Brooklands, and one afternoon took my mother for a ride in a 'pusher' biplane which had basketwork seats on the lower wings. When my mother returned home and excitedly reported her exploit to her strictly Victorian parents, she was sent to her room for a week on bread and water!

At the beginning of World War I armed forces were developing both balloons and fixed wing airplanes as an adjunct to their operations. The exigencies of the war after only four years were followed by a rapid general development of aircraft which in June 1919, a few months after the war ended, enabled the successful crossing of the Atlantic by Alcock and Brown from Newfoundland to Ireland using a Vickers Vimy bomber and taking about sixteen and a half hours. In 1927 an American colonel, Charles Lindbergh, made the first solo Atlantic crossing direct from the United States to Paris in a flimsy single engine monoplane known as the *Spirit of St Louis*.

In the United Kingdom there were many ex-service airplanes and pilots available and short flights were offered to the general public for as little as 5/- (five shillings – 25 pence in today's money) per 'flip', using beaches and fields as makeshift airstrips. Flying clubs appeared all over the country, mostly conducted from suitable grass fields adjacent to which hangars and club premises could be and were built. Silvio de Moyse Bucknall, the headmaster of my prep school, Brightlands of Dulwich Common, had been in the Royal Flying Corps in World War I, piloting two-seater Bristol Fighters, and was a member of the Redhill Flying Club south of London. When I was twelve or thirteen years old, he taught me the rudiments of flying at that club in one of the immediate predecessors of the Tiger Moth, which itself became the basic trainer for many World War II pilots. It had two cockpits. I sat in the front, and my headmaster shouted instructions through a voice tube. All aspects of these flying escapades of mine were insured at Lloyd's by my father who was a senior executive of Willis Faber.

It was not long before there were regular air services between London (Croydon) and Paris and other European destinations, as well as between many cities in the United States. The development of this form of travel was remarkable in the period up to 1939. For long-distance flights the flying boat was the master. The Americans were using 'Clipper' flying boats across the Atlantic to Europe and across the Pacific to the Far East. The British were offering passenger services to South Africa, India, the Far East and Australasia using 'Empire' flying boats built by Shorts. During World War II the 'Empire' was developed into the 'Sunderland', a most successful maritime reconnaissance and U-boat hunter which played a major role in the Battle of the Atlantic. The

Supermarine S6B, an attractive looking sea plane, was built for the Schneider Trophy Race. On its third successive win it retained the trophy outright for Britain. It was from this machine that the Spitfire evolved, with Lloyd's being concerned at every stage either by way of direct insurance or reinsurance.

An aeronautical development which received a large boost during World War I was the rigid dirigible airship, notably those built at Freidrichshafen by Count von Zeppelin, an officer of the German army. These craft carried out bombardments over the East Coast of England and London. After the war ended, the Germans continued production of these airships for civilian purposes, as did the British and the Americans, the latter's most successful being the *Akron* and the *Macon*. The British had a series designated *R* with a number following, notably *R100* and *R101*. The *R101* crashed in France on its maiden commercial flight to India. The Germans continued with this luxurious form of air travel with the *Graf Zeppelin* which operated regularly between Europe and North and South America, ceasing only when the *Hindenburg*, after more than sixty flights to the United States without undue incident, burst into flames whilst approaching its mooring mast in New Jersey in May 1937. The German Zeppelins used hydrogen to provide the lift. Hydrogen is the lightest gas but it is also highly inflammable. The Americans in their development of airships used helium which is non-combustible, so the fire hazard as such was not a serious integral problem; but helium is heavier relative to hydrogen and therefore volume to volume it provides proportionately less lifting power.

During World War II tethered balloons were used by the British as a defence against low-flying aircraft and, more importantly, for the initial training of the army's parachute soldiers. In 1946, Lloyd's provided a Comprehensive Personal Accident cover for all airborne reserve forces which protected such individuals including their military activities. Over 95 per cent of claims did not involve parachuting, use of explosives, mountaineering, or exercises with live ammunition, but were connected with recreational activities – such as football! I was protected in my Territorial Army service under this policy but made no claim.

A most successful aircraft, the Douglas DC3, also known as

the C54 or the 'Dakota', which, since its development from its predecessor the DC2, a very good passenger aeroplane, was probably the air equivalent of the Jeep, the Bailey bridge and Liberty ships as successful tools in the winning of World War II. Many thousands of DC3s were built and took part in operations worldwide such as Burma with the Chindits, supplying the Chinese over the 'Hump', and D-Day, Arnhem, crossing the Rhine, and later the Berlin Airlift. They were tough enough to lift off from makeshift airfields by using JATO (Jet-Assisted Take-Off) bottles attached to the aircraft which allowed an astonishing take-off performance (amazingly the aircraft stayed in one piece – I experienced this once and it scared the pants off me!). It was similar to taking off in a two-seat jet fighter. The DC3 was also a popular aircraft with parachute soldiers. A few are still in use in various parts of the world. They were often referred to as the married pilot's or insurance man's best friend.

The influence of the two World Wars contributed greatly in the twentieth century to the development of aviation generally, and after World War II aviation continued to advance at a phenomenal rate through the introduction of the jet engine originally developed by Sir Frank Whittle immediately prior to and during the war. Without that engine, international flights as we know them today would not have been possible. The American Boeing 707, the Douglas DC8 and the Lockheed Electra were the most widely used, although the Lockheed Electra was not a pure jet but a turboprop. The British developed a very beautiful looking pure jet, the De Havilland Comet which, after one or two initial disasters due to pressurisation problems giving rise to metal fatigue, went on to become a useful passenger aeroplane and, indeed, its Royal Air Force version has for many years seen service as an excellent maritime reconnaissance aircraft known as 'Nimrod'. The British also developed the Vickers Viscount turboprop, many of which went into service throughout the world. The British VC10 and Super VC10 were *very successful* passenger aircraft, which subsequently became tankers and transports used by the Royal Air Force.

In the late 1940s when air travel was becoming accepted as the norm, slot machine Personal Accident Flight Insurance was established. The brokers who initiated this useful service, with Lloyd's as the insurer, employed a man whose duty it was to visit airports in southern England to collect the cash premiums and copies of individual insurance certificates purchased, and to generally service the machines. This person happened to be having an affair with the wife of a businessman who made frequent trips by air to the Continent. Upon learning that the aircraft in which his paramour's husband was travelling had crashed, he visited a slot machine at the airport and inserted appropriate details and cash. The widow collected a substantial amount of insurance. Unfortunately for the pair of them, this nasty little opportunistic fraud came to light.

The helicopter, a development from the 1930s Cierva Autogyro, also 'took off' at an astounding rate. I remember, in 1951, after spending a weekend with my Territorial Army Unit, during which we were introduced to the helicopter, talking to a leading Aviation underwriter at Lloyd's about this experience, and he commented that the helicopter would never be of any practical civilian use! Having crossed the Atlantic many times on business by air, including Concorde, and having used such facilities as the helicopter platforms in the heart of New York City and elsewhere, and frequently flown by helicopter from Penzance to the Isles of Scilly on holiday, and travelled from Battersea Heliport to Epsom Races, I know it would be very foolish for anyone at any time to say that something new is unlikely to develop into anything useful, or to say that a project of any kind is impossible. Helicopters are now the most versatile of all aircraft – as ambulances, in police activities, rescues (sea, mountains, tops of burning buildings, lifting out of awkward places), taxis, media uses, and so on ad infinitum.

The British Vertical Take-Off and Landing aircraft (VTOL) evolved from a simple but incredibly strange-looking framework known most appropriately as the 'Flying Bedstead' into the highly sophisticated 'Harrier' Jump Jet, which has seen successful war service and has great possible civilian potential.

World War II witnessed the development by the Germans of the V2, a delivery vehicle of high explosive by rocket. After the war, many scientists and engineers involved in this project, notably Werner von Braun who became an American citizen, joined the American scientists in the development of military rockets which formed the nucleus of the National Aeronautical and Space Administration (NASA), now responsible for all American space activities.

Aviation, in the broadest definition of the word, opened a huge new area of insurance and this void was filled primarily by Lloyd's underwriters, Marine and Non-Marine, who continued to write it as such alongside specialist Aviation underwriters, and also by specialist insurance companies, most notably the British Aviation Insurance Company. It is not only the aircraft themselves with hulls becoming even larger and more expensive which require insurance: there are all the Third Party Liabilities involved – aircraft manufacturers, passengers, cargoes, airline and airport operators, traffic controllers, pilots, flying clubs, gliding clubs, travel tour operators, and so on.

Supersonic flying produced another interesting aspect of insurance. This was the noise known as a sonic boom which occurs in the vicinity of anything travelling faster than the speed of sound. Anybody who has been in the butts below the targets on a two hundred or five hundred yards rifle range will have experienced the oddity of hearing the 'crack-thump', the 'crack' being generated by the bullet passing overhead and the 'thump' being the actual sound of the rifle firing which catches up a second or two later. The 'crack' from something as small as a rifle bullet does not cause any harm per se, but if the 'crack' was generated by something as large as an aeroplane then the resultant 'crack' or noise can become a heavy sonic boom which may cause damage on the ground to panes of glass in homes and greenhouses, and also disturb farm or other animals.

Most 'All Risks' insurances now include damage from sonic boom. Although I know that claims have been made in respect of this peril, I have not been involved in any personally, but remember in the 1960s when the prototype Concordes were being tested at supersonic speeds down the Irish Sea there were complaints from people who heard the boom and claimed that they had damage caused by it. Apparently, Concorde's manufacturers tried an experiment. It is alleged that they announced the date and time of the next supersonic flight down the Irish Sea. Sure enough, complaints of damage flooded in. The only problem was that Concorde was deliberately grounded that day. I cannot vouch for the truth of this, but it does make a good and very plausible story.

What a beautiful aircraft Concorde is. From personal experience, it is certainly the best way to fly between London and New York or Washington without suffering from jet lag. Going from east to west and using local time differences, passengers arrive before their time of departure. Travelling in the opposite direction is the equivalent of a rather long lunch. It is to be hoped that when Concorde is finally retired, there will be another generation of supersonic passenger aircraft to take its place.

Aviation has minimised the time spans of distances, and this was brought home to me very forcibly when flying for the first time across Canada, which was at night. I noticed a small cluster of lights on the ground, perhaps five or six, then nothing for about twenty minutes until another small cluster of lights appeared – which at over four hundred miles an hour meant we had travelled nearly two hundred miles. It looked very lonely down there.

Getting into Lloyd's

How did one get into Lloyd's?

When I joined Lloyd's, recruiting for this organisation was similar to that of any other City of London financial institution. There were several approaches, and I am talking generally about staff of any kind. There would be advertisements and personal introductions. The former produced the vast proportion of the clerical staff, whether they were in the underwriting, broking or Lloyd's administrative areas. My own employment was by way of my father introducing me to his broking firm, Willis Faber, in which he was a senior executive, and I discovered that many of my contemporaries at Lloyd's, both brokers and underwriters, had also been recruited through personal introductions.

However, a great many highly successful people were recruited almost by accident. A very important and influential leading underwriter, after leaving school at the age of fourteen, had been employed first as a messenger boy by a broking company: an underwriter was impressed by the boy and invited him to join him on his box. His career progressed from that moment. Another senior underwriter when a lad of about fifteen years old was selling newspapers outside Lloyd's: a pen underwriter who bought his papers from him invited him to join him on his box. Yet again, there was a lad employed in a sandwich bar near Lloyd's who took the same route. These three gentlemen, starting literally on the bottom rung without having personally approached Lloyd's, reached the top of the ladder by their own ability but, of course, their school days had not been wasted by a 'progressive' education. They had all received what used to be referred to as an elementary education and were therefore fully competent in reading, writing, basic mathematics, and common sense, unlike some of today's school leavers.

An observation regarding employment at Lloyd's and national service is worth mentioning. I was not a conscript myself, having volunteered during World War II as soon as I was eighteen. I served for over six years as a full-time soldier, and for a long time afterwards in the Territorial Army. On my return to civilian life, aged twenty-four, it was noticeable to me that I was at a disadvantage because the best 'learning years' of my life had been lost. I had to work and study very hard to catch up. Later, it was very interesting to see how young persons who had joined the company at age fifteen or sixteen as junior clerks, messenger boys, or assistants in the post department, had matured during the two years when they were away doing their national service. The differences were incredible. From callow youths they had become confident young men eligible for advancement in the company with the ultimate aim of working on their own initiative in the Lloyd's market. Paradoxically, I do not support the principle of national service in the armed forces, if only because our professional soldiers, who are the best in the world, cannot be lumbered with thousands of recruits who leave just when they are becoming useful. This is not intended to cast a slur on the many superb conscripts who served with great credit and bravery, many of whom lost their lives on active service during the years that national service was in existence. However, I do believe very strongly that responsible employers should encourage their staff to join the active reserve forces.

The broker community consisted of a dozen or so large firms with international accounts, and many others of various sizes. After a few years of working in this community, a broker would know all the underwriters and brokers in his own Marine, Non-Marine, Aviation or other market and most of those in sister markets. Individual career structures and prospects were basically simple and straightforward. There were many who, once having obtained a middle position in the broking set-up, had no ambition to go further. This was of benefit to a large employer because important but sedentary positions were safely filled by people who were quite happy in their repetitive jobs and content to stay where they were.

Personal movements within the broking community, although slow, were generally vertical, especially in the large firms. There was a lateral movement, but usually an experienced person might move from a large firm to a relatively more senior position in a smaller firm. Movement to similar positions between brokers was an infrequent happening. Movements from brokers to underwriting boxes were fairly common but quite rare the other way, although it did happen. An underwriting deputy might move to become the pen underwriter on a different box. Previously planned or – to use a stronger word – 'plotted' movements would have caused a flutter in the hen coop. 'Moves' were always discussed between firms' principals and the 'moving parties' in a gentlemanly manner. I experienced this on two occasions but declined these flattering offers because I enjoyed what I was doing.

So that was the overall picture, operating in a very relaxed and civilised manner. This conduct, practice, call it what you will, worked well and helped to maintain a high all-round standard of integrity which benefited all concerned – Names, underwriting agents, underwriting staff, brokers, insureds, and reinsureds. In so doing, it preserved the good name of that part of the London insurance market centred on Lloyd's and supported by the 'fringe' company market.

As Lloyd's and the City of London insurance market in general developed, it became a kind of 'club' in the best meaning of that word and encompassed all those persons working in the insurance business. The principle of 'Utmost Good Faith' was accepted and obeyed without question. This 'club' had evolved over a period of some three hundred years and there was no reason to suppose it would not continue its proper development for a similar amount of time. Unfortunately, such a supposition takes no account of that most indeterminate factor – human nature.

The Underwriting Member

From the first day of my employment in the community of Lloyd's I was aware that I was in one of several distinct groups within its confines. I was one of many who again were split roughly in half – those on the underwriting side and those on the broking side – but, of course, I soon realised that there were many of a somewhat amorphous group who did neither one nor the other but who kept the whole thing running, the Corporation of Lloyd's and its own employees. Not only that, but it soon became apparent there was another mysterious group known as 'underwriting members', also known as 'Names', without the presence of whom I was assured Lloyd's could not exist. The working capital of Lloyd's was unique and totally different from that of any other financial business concept.

The capital of an insurance company comes from shareholders who buy stock in the company and hopefully expect to get a dividend on their investments at the end of each year. Alternatively, the capital of a mutual company is not owned by outside stockholders but by those who are participating in the business themselves. A stock life insurance company has shareholders who have nothing whatsoever to do with life insurance in their day-to-day lives other than possibly having a personal life insurance policy, in the same way as shareholders in other corporations have no involvement in the day-to-day management of their companies except possibly buying their cars or other products. A mutual life insurance company is owned by the policyholders as is any other class of mutual insurance company. At no time could an investor or shareholder in a stock company lose more than his original subscription or investment. It is possible for a mutual company to have a 'call', or request for money, on its policyholders, but if its reinsurance programme is well structured such an occurrence would be most unlikely.

The 'working capital' of Lloyd's was provided not by shareholders in the normal sense of that word, but by individuals who are best described as 'sole traders' in the same way that each stallholder in a street market is a sole trader. The stallholder is permitted, or licensed, to trade by the local authority in a particular area, street market, or wherever. Underwriting members of Lloyd's are permitted to trade in The Room at Lloyd's.

Regulations for so doing having developed over the years were laid down by the Corporation of Lloyd's which was managed by the Committee of Lloyd's (now known as the Council of Lloyd's). Although each underwriting member is technically and legally a sole trader, it would be impossible if they all turned up at The Room to conduct business, especially when the number of underwriting members approached 35,000. Furthermore, only a tiny fraction of underwriting members had the remotest idea of how their personal assets were being used, not to mention the complexities of the insurance and reinsurance business in which they had willingly and wholeheartedly become involved. Nevertheless, these people were very happy to tell the world that they were 'underwriting members or Names at Lloyd's' – it carried great prestige. There was even one eccentric whose personal card was printed with just his name and 'Lloyd's, London'. His mail always reached him.

Amongst the various activities of the Committee of Lloyd's its prime duty was to ensure that the security behind any Lloyd's policy was beyond question, and only secondarily should the interests of individual underwriting members or their underwriting agents be of any concern to the Committee of Lloyd's unless, of course, should fraud or other criminal or dubious activities be involved, including those of brokers. By the same token, other activities conducted in the City of London have similar applications. The committees of the Corporation of London, for example, which control Billingsgate, Leadenhall, Smithfield, and Spitalfields Markets, are not responsible for the financial well-being of any of the traders, their partners, shareholders, and so on – but are responsible for the proper general conduct of their activities, and for the safety, etc., of the products supplied and the premises from which they are dispensed. To emphasise this point, it was not a duty of the Committee of Lloyd's to protect the individual Name from his underwriting activities – far less to compensate him if they went wrong. Personal Stop Loss insurance was available to any member or Name to take care of that contingency. In the City of London, traders in Billingsgate and Leadenhall Markets or their shareholders would not dream of attacking the committees which regulate their market activities to recompense them for incompetent trading. If your car is a disaster you do not sue the Society of Motor Manufacturers and Traders for compensation. So why should a Name blame Lloyd's as such for his misjudged investment in certain syndicates which he chose after discussions with, amongst others, his members agency and financial advisers?

How did these underwriting members become involved in the first place? The only proper answer can be by reputation and/or word of mouth. Joe Blow might be chatting to John Doe at his club, in the pub, or anywhere else for that matter. John Doe is an underwriting member. Joe Blow is not. John might casually suggest to Joe, whom he knows to be a very wealthy person, that he should consider entering the community known as underwriting membership at Lloyd's. Or Joe might ask John how one became an underwriting member. A vital difference between this and normal investments is that there could never be a 'prospectus' of any kind which one would usually expect to be available for studying prior to entering into any serious financial commitment.

The chain from prospective to actual underwriting member of Lloyd's (and we will take it that Joe has never had anything to do with Lloyd's) is that he is first introduced to a members agency. Upon joining the members agency, it will 'offer' him to managing (also known as underwriting) agencies. (The term 'members agency' was always to me somewhat amorphous and could be everything or nothing to a Name. My members agency was also my underwriting agency so I could not see the necessity for having this extra organisation in the chain. Nobody ever explained to me what members agencies contributed to the overall benefit of Lloyd's. In my view they appeared to do very little for a Name that could not have been included in the activities of the Name's underwriting agency.)

It must be explained to the prospective member that there are very serious financial considerations. This will be done by the members agency, his managing agent(s), and finally by the Rota Committee, a duty sub-committee of the Council of Lloyd's.

The considerations varied over the years. The usual basic requirements were a wealth certificate of £75,000 and this was expected to consist of good stocks and shares. Real estate values were not allowed. The certificate would have to be brought up to date, year by year. A deposit of £25,000 would be handed to the Committee of Lloyd's and this deposit had to be in Lloyd's approved securities. However, the member would continue to receive dividends off the securities he had deposited. In other words, his deposit was held in trust by the Committee of Lloyds. Hence the oft quoted expression, 'By this means your money will work for you twice.' Using this example, the overall premium income – Marine, Non-Marine, Aviation, etc. – permitted to be underwritten by the 'pen underwriter(s)' on behalf of the new Name would be £150,000, i.e., twice the value of his wealth certificate. Which syndicate or syndicates to join was entirely between the prospective member and his members and underwriting agencies. The Committee of Lloyd's would take no part in this specific aspect.

Premium income limit is the overall total of the amounts of premiums accredited to a Name each year. A simple example. A pen underwriter for a syndicate with five hundred Names puts his line of, say, 10 per cent on a risk with an annual premium of $400,000. He will be taking in $40,000 on behalf of his Names. Assume that each of his Names has an equal share. Then each will have $80 credited to his personal account for that risk, and, of course, the same proportion to pay in the event that the risk becomes a loss. However, all the Names of a given syndicate will not necessarily have the same shares.

Our new prospective member, having disclosed his assets and arranged for his deposit to be transferred into the custody or trusteeship of Lloyd's, will be invited to attend the Rota Committee for final approval. At this meeting it will be explained in great detail that a percentage of his premium income will go into the Central Fund, which is solely for the benefit of all holders of insurance policies issued by Lloyd's and in no way for that of underwriting members. Secondly, and most important, and this will be expressed quite clearly, his *entire personal assets*, not just the value of his wealth certificate, will be at risk and available to pay losses on those policies upon which his name appears as a participant. In other words, he is entering into an agreement which subjects him to absolute unlimited personal liability for his underwriting activities as a sole trader 'down to his last shirt stud', as has so often been quoted. It is as simple as that.

The foregoing sets out the basics for an underwriting member, but there were many variations where some underwriting members were underwriting to very much greater limits, say between £500,000 and £1 million premium income with appropriate deposits and wealth certificates. Also, there were variations depending upon whether the Name was a 'working' Name whose normal business activities were at Lloyd's or whether he was an 'outside' Name as in the case of Joe Blow. If his assets and/or deposits were sufficient, he could be enrolled with many more than just one managing agent.

In 1950 there were 2,743 Names at Lloyd's, almost all of whom were 'real' with wealth certificates. However, there were a few so-called 'sponsored' Names with no wealth certificates and deposits of only £8,000 which could have been loaned by their employers, or anyone else for that matter. At this time there were only a few hundred or so pen underwriters actually putting pen to paper. A syndicate of a hundred Names was considered large, and there were some with as few as half a dozen Names. During the course of my first twenty years working at Lloyd's, my employers on no less than three occasions offered to put me up as a 'sponsored' Name. All I needed was £8,000 as a deposit with no wealth certificate requirement but, of course, acceptance of unlimited personal liability in respect of underwriting activities arranged on my behalf. Furthermore, if I did not have access to £8,000 for the deposit, they would lend it to me and this loan would be paid back out of my underwriting profits (if any!). I was very grateful but declined with thanks. To me this went against the whole principle of underwriting membership of Lloyd's. With this tiny deposit of mine, no one was able to explain to me what would happen if my syndicate made huge losses on my behalf, or who would pay them. My underwriting agency? The broking company who employed me and loaned me my deposit? Or other underwriting members through the Central Fund?

In the early 1970s, Lord Cromer's recommendation of a reduction in the minimum wealth certificate from £75,000 to £37,500, with appropriate reductions in deposits and premium income limits, made it possible for many to 'qualify' as 'proper' underwriting members known as 'Mini Names'. Nevertheless, the introduction of the 'Mini Names' category did not take care of the already existing problem of 'Sponsored Names'. In a period of rapidly increasing inflation this idea did not seem to make sense to me. However, being prudent, I took advantage of this new situation and joined as a 'Mini Name' (although by that time I was able to become a full-blown Name with a £75,000 wealth certificate). I maintained all my deposit securities in short dated gilts which meant that my deposit and actual wealth were increasing slowly all the time. I insisted that my underwriting agents transferred the maximum permitted of any underwriting profits into what is known as Special Reserve, which has certain tax advantages and is an additional personal safeguard.

I also purchased a Personal Stop Loss reinsurance which, when I first became a Name, was very cheap. There were many variations. My particular Stop Loss protected me should I be asked for money at the end of an underwriting year, and would pay excess of the first £5,000 that was asked of me. Such a policy would have a limit and I picked the figure of £25,000, which was then a substantial sum. Should my underwriting results for a certain year, instead of giving me a profit, result in my being asked for, say, £35,000 – which would have been most unlikely in those days – I would have paid the first £5,000, my Stop Loss the next £25,000, and I would be liable for the balance. This, of course, would be in respect of my underwriting account for that year. I understand that some pen underwriters discouraged their Names from buying Personal Stop Loss reinsurance as it would constitute a slur on their underwriting abilities!

The Lloyd's accounting system working on a three-year cycle required any one accounting year to be 'closed' at the end of its third year. The resulting profit or loss would be the first entry in the next three-year cycle. Thus a completely new underwriting member on any syndicate would start his first year with a chunk of premium. If he was unlucky the first entry in his account for that year could be a loss. However, this did not matter unless he was unfortunate enough to be on a syndicate where his underwriter's accountants could not 'close' the year because outstanding liabilities, including incurred but not reported losses, were not available or it was not possible for them to be calculated on a reasonable basis. This is known as 'reinsurance to close' – that is to say, the result at the end of one year, be it a profit or a loss of a syndicate, is 'reinsured' into the next year. If it was not possible to calculate the 'reinsurance to close', such a year would become what is known as an open year, and it follows that the longer the year remained 'open' the more that year's accounts would deteriorate, because losses shown in that year could not be transferred into succeeding years. This would be serious in the case of a syndicate writing a large proportion of 'Long Tail' business, that is to say, Third Party Liability insurance of any kind, especially Products Liability.

I felt safe in my underwriting membership, as my underwriting agency and the firm for whom I worked as a broker were part of a very large and successful financial conglomerate in the City of London and elsewhere, each part of which could and naturally did assist the others. The agency itself formed only a very small part of this overall group. On the other hand, the agency benefited for many reasons by being part of it. For example, the group had a Company Security Section which employed a unit whose sole task was to look into the financial soundness of insurance and other companies generally. If my underwriting agents were offered reinsurance by any broker in the market, they only had to lift up the telephone to get a reliable update on the financial security of the reinsurance being offered. Investments of the underwriting funds and premiums would be properly looked after as part of a very large portfolio, including overnight deposits on cash flows. This worked most satisfactorily for many, many years. A totally independent underwriting agency would not have such good back-up resources, although some independent agencies were very successful.

Also, at that time, the Committee of Lloyd's had what was known as the Twenty Per Cent Rule which permitted only 20 per cent of each of the many individual components of Lloyd's to be owned by foreigners. This was a very important factor in a complicated business enterprise or market in which the integrity of the personalities involved was paramount to its successful operation.

On several occasions I was approached by outsiders about membership and I always responded in the same way. One of these approaches was of more than usual interest. I had a telephone call from a personal friend who was an American insurance broker. He asked if I knew Mr XYZ. I did. Mr XYZ was an important pen underwriter at Lloyd's. My friend said, 'I'm calling you because this gentleman, a total stranger, came into my office today completely out of the blue and told me that as some of my business was being underwritten at Lloyd's he thought it was time I became an underwriting member.'

As I knew he was visiting London the following week, I said I would arrange for him to meet several managing agents, including my own, but that in each case he should ask the following minimum number of questions:

a. What were the underwriting results for each of the last ten to fifteen years?

b. What were and are the syndicate's reinsurance programmes?

c. By whom are the reinsurance programmes underwritten?

d. How long has the senior pen underwriter been with the syndicate?

e. Does the syndicate's proposed underwriting differ from that of its previous years?

f. What is and what was the syndicate's proportion of 'Long Tail' to 'Short Tail' business?

g. How has the number of its Names grown or diminished over the last few years, and does that have any significance?

h. Are there, or have there been, any outstanding 'open years'?

I suggested that when he had obtained the answers to these questions, he should discuss the matter with Le Boeufs, Lloyd's attorneys in New York (not for UK prospective members), his accountants, his financial advisers – and then, 'Don't do it! But, if you still insist, I am prepared to sign your application papers.' I also advised him very strongly to buy Personal Stop Loss reinsurances for each separate syndicate underwriting year of account, with substantial limits to take care of possible open years and the complications that could arise therefrom.

He took the plunge.

So What Went Wrong?

The overall 'profit' or 'loss' at 'Lloyd's' for anyone year represents the aggregates of all the Names' results – profits or losses – and a year showing a healthy *'profit'* or *'loss'* for *'Lloyd's'* could and did represent *fat profits* for some Names and *substantial losses* for others, with many variations in between. Those in the former group would regard their Lloyd's membership as having had a good year. Those in the latter group would regard their Lloyd's membership as having had a bad year. It being a marketplace, some traders might have a succession or alternation of good and bad years depending upon the skills of their underwriting agents together with the overall luck of the worldwide insurance and reinsurance business.

What did go wrong?

When I first joined the broking side of Lloyd's there existed within the marketplace several hundred underwriting syndicates of all sizes, some totally independent, some attached to broking houses, some grouped together under one underwriting agency, and some attached to more than one underwriting agency. There were about 230 accredited broking firms or houses ranging from very large to very small. Some small firms were very specialised and remarkably successful. During my time, individual underwriting organisations merged or enlarged, as did broking organisations. On both the underwriting and broking sides this was all part of a natural progression of market forces. Many of these firms have now either completely disappeared or partially changed their names reflecting mergers and acquisitions. Currently there are only three major brokers – AON, Marsh, and Willis – plus about 125 smaller broking firms, many of which will undoubtedly merge. I do not consider this to have been a healthy development for a marketplace such as Lloyd's, which was dependent upon strong but friendly competition coupled with the proper and natural arrival of new blood. It weakened the innovative disposition of those involved to the detriment of all, not least the policyholders. Hopefully, this situation will be only temporary.

Before considering the recent problems, an historical look back first to the early 1920s is needed to set the scene. A man named Harrison, a pen underwriter with just a few Names, was using an involved procedure to guarantee hire purchase agreements on motor vehicles. It became a financial disaster. The Committee of Lloyd's under the chairmanship of A. L. Sturge, together with the Brokers Association, paid Harrison's Names' losses. From this point the Lloyd's Central Fund was formally established, being built up from a percentage levy on all underwriting members' premiums. The fund was to be used explicitly for protecting policyholders from defaulting individual Names, and for no other purpose.

In 1954 another financial problem occurred when A. E. M. Wilcox, who was both a small broker and a small underwriting agent, 'ran into difficulties'. None of Wilcox's policyholders suffered and all creditors were paid in full. What it amounted to was a fraudulent broker/underwriter 'acquiring' a fraudulent auditor, a most unusual combination which led to the syndicate's default. Lloyd's decided that the Names on Wilcox's syndicate should be relieved of their underwriting debts.

In the latter half of the 1970s came what was known as the 'Sasse Affair'. This was a complicated and unsavoury business and can best be described as a combination of factors including the misuse of binding authorities. North American agents who had not been approved by Lloyd's were issuing insurance certificates off a binding authority, 'underwritten' by the Sasse syndicate, which had not been properly documented through the Lloyd's Policy Signing Office. The risks concerned were mostly of the 'distress' type – typically, run-down buildings in run-down districts – and were certainly not of the type that would be willingly underwritten by a prudent insurer which knew what it was doing. An additional complication was that the business was reinsured by a well-known and very reputable international reinsurer, the Instituto Reaseguros Do Brasil, which became unhappy. Also, there were some strange and dubious individuals involved in the chain, from the owners of the insured properties via brokers on both sides of the Atlantic to Sasse, and thence to the reinsurer. Some time before this unfortunate saga broke, I was travelling in the United States when several of my friends in the insurance business told me about 'dreadful' Fire Property Damage insurances being issued in the name of Lloyd's. I reported this at length to the appropriate authorities on my return. I also made extensive personal enquiries in the marketplace, but the one underwriter I did not approach was Tim Sasse as it was common knowledge that his syndicate did not write North American Property Damage business. It was never clear, certainly not to me, what he did underwrite – other than obscure 'one-off' deals arranged in his office. He never accepted any business I offered him. Unfortunately, Tim was easily flattered and seemed unable to recognise the dangers implicit in such a susceptibility. I was on good terms with him. He had been awarded a Military Cross when serving with the Ghurkhas in Italy, and we had been fellow officers together in the Territorial Army. I don't think he really settled in at Lloyd's after leaving the army. He had a share in a syndicate (horse racing, not Lloyd's) which owned a horse named Rheingold, the winner in 1973 of the French Prix de L'Arc de Triomphe, the richest race in the French calendar. Rheingold was subsequently sold for about a million pounds. I had the feeling Tim was much happier being with the racing fraternity than at Lloyd's in the underwriting/broking community.

The Sasse Affair cost a great deal of money for the Names involved on their 1976 and 1977 years of account. The overall loss was something in excess of £20 million, of which the Corporation of Lloyd's contributed around £15 million which was, in fact, 'peanuts' (to use an American expression) in comparison to what later hit Lloyd's. It is not clear whether this sum came from the Central Fund or from other funds held by the Corporation.

Now, let's look at some selected figures.

In 1948 there were 2,422 Names. The overall premium income in respect of all classes for that year was £125 million, which produced an overall profit of £19.5 million or just under 15½ per cent, despite the fact that there was an unusual November windstorm which hit most of the East Coast states of America.

By 1965 the number of Names had more than doubled to 5,554. The overall premium income had risen to £461 million which produced an overall loss of nearly £38 million (-8.2 per cent). The following two years' results were: premiums of £531 million in 1966 and £601 million in 1967, with losses of £18.5 million and £1.5 million (-3.5 per cent and -0.27 per cent), respectively. These successive three years' results undoubtedly reflected the Lloyd's three-year accounting system coupled with the very heavy losses in 1965 caused by the North American and Caribbean Hurricane 'Betsy', the overall cost of which to Lloyd's and all other insurers was $1,420 million.

By 1969 the number of Names had increased slightly to 6,042 and the premium income had risen to just under £694 million which produced an overall profit of £52 million (7.5 per cent) in spite of Hurricane 'Camille', the overall cost of which was similar to that of 'Betsy' in 1965.

But by 1982 the number of Names had risen to 20,145. Why? And how? The overall premium income had risen to just over £6 billion and the overall profit for that year was £57 million (.92 per cent).

It should be re-emphasised that these figures represented large losses for some Names but good or substantial profits for other Names. During the 1980s I was becoming uneasy about the way Lloyd's was expanding. In 1975, my first year of underwriting, there were about 7,000 Names. By the late 1980s the number was over 30,000. It looked to me like a very unhealthy expansion. This, plus the accelerating number of disasters that were taking place throughout the world which involved Lloyd's, prompted me to decide that I should cease to be an underwriting member. Unfortunately, at the same time, I was told I had an open year on a Marine syndicate because it had started to dabble in underwriters' Excess of Loss reinsurances, known as 'LMXs' – which were accelerating into a nasty spiral of losses going from one underwriting syndicate to another at fractions of the real or indeed the original underwriting price. The only winners in this ludicrous situation were the reinsurance brokers. Up until then I had assumed that my Marine underwriter would be underwriting Marine business – not taking in other underwriters' 'dirty washing', including Non-Marine, by underwriting LMXs. That last underwriting year also included my share in the 1988 Piper Alpha Oil Rig loss which itself went into the LMX spiral. But, luckily for me, my underwriting agents resolved this problem and I was able to come out of all liabilities at Lloyd's and receive back my deposit and most of my Special Reserve. I did not even have to call upon my Personal Stop Loss reinsurance. My underwriting membership was, overall, a successful, if risky, business. On my £75,000 permitted annual premium income I received an average return of about £7,000, as much as possible of which was put into Special Reserve. This reserve more than looked after my final year which contained the serious loss from my Marine syndicate causing the 'open year' just mentioned.

When glancing through the annual publication listing Names and their syndicates, it surprised me that many Names had not only their spouses but also their offspring listed. I used to ask, 'Surely only one member of a family can undertake the responsibilities of unlimited personal liability? How would the creditors be split up?' I was told, as it didn't concern me personally, to mind my own business!

Problems emerged in the late 1960s and during the 1970s, 1980s and 1990s involving various personalities, underwriting agencies, and broking companies, not to mention 'offshore companies' used for 'reinsurance purposes' in Bermuda, Panama, the Cayman Islands, Gibraltar, Switzerland, Liechtenstein, Guernsey, the Isle of Man, and so on. Also, a number of the London so-called 'fringe market' insurance companies ran into difficulties and/or disappeared from the scene. All of which gave many of us who were at the sharp end of insurance broking and underwriting very serious cause for concern. The individual persons and organisations and their respective antics have been well covered by many writers and investigative journalists, and do not need any further comment.

At the same time, Lloyd's was being subjected to a barrage of horrendous losses from the Third Party Liability sector involving asbestosis, pneumoconiosis, and the effects of Agent Orange which was used as a defoliant during the Vietnam War, to name just a few of the more important. Also, there was a series of disasters both natural and man-made, including ice storms, floods, windstorms, earthquakes, the computer leasing fiasco which concerned heavy losses on contingency insurances in respect of computer leasing contracts being cancelled, and so on. These disasters triggered off a rush of Names voluntarily resigning from membership, together with both new and long-standing Names being faced with ever-increasing losses and imponderables. Of course, no Names could resign and get totally clear if their accounts had any 'open years': they were locked in until such open years were properly 'closed'.

I was intrigued by the practice which grew up whereby when offering a nice piece of business to an underwriter, after agreeing his line he might ask my permission to include an extra amount on behalf of his so-called 'baby syndicate' which had a separate syndicate number. I believe that it had the effect of feeding certain Names of an underwriting syndicate with extra cream off the business. I may be quite wrong about all this but it still nags at me. Otherwise, what was the point of having a baby syndicate and under what rule of the Committee or Council of Lloyd's did it fall?

The most seriously worrying occurrence to me was when Lloyd's appeared to have broken its Twenty Per Cent Rule which barred foreigners from owning more than 20 per cent of any Lloyd's broking or underwriting organisation. As an underwriting member I queried this in writing with the then chairman of Lloyd's, and was given a very rude rebuff, which was supported by fellow directors in my own company, and I was, again, told to mind my own business.

Two of the largest brokers are now foreign owned – AON and Marsh, the latter having taken over C. T. Bowring.

Another very damaging development, as far as I and many others were concerned, was that broking organisations were instructed by Lloyd's to divest themselves of any underwriting activities – a condition imposed by Parliament during the passage of the Bill if Lloyd's was to get the 1982 Act. The Council of Lloyd's had no alternative.

There was a lot of ill-informed comment employing again that usefully vague and 'in' expression 'conflict of interest', which can mean anything or nothing depending upon how and when it is used – a real cliché. Also, about this time, one or two large independent underwriting syndicates, and by that I mean not connected with or owned by brokers, decided to have the shares in their agencies quoted on the Stock Exchange. In other words, they 'went public'. This struck me as being somewhat questionable because those who put up the capital which supported the agencies were individual Names, accepting totally unlimited personal liability, and were the only persons who should share in underwriting profits (if any) except, of course, those employed within the agencies themselves.

I discussed this at the time with many people, who pointed out that the underwriting agency within which I was a member was indirectly quoted on the Stock Exchange. This was true to a certain extent. My underwriting agency formed only a very small part of a large and successful conglomerate of financial interests covering many aspects of businesses in the City of London and elsewhere. It did have compensating factors. The underwriting agency itself benefited for a number of reasons by being part of this financial group, and the arrangement worked satisfactorily for many, many years. A totally independent underwriting agency could not possibly have had such good back-up financial resources and expertise. I was very disturbed when, because of the 1982 Act, my underwriting agency was ordered by Lloyd's to be divested from its parent financial group and had to go out on its own. I felt like a yachtsman who found that his life jackets had been removed from his vessel.

At this point I began to get more forebodings, particularly as over the years there had been a gradual and then suddenly accelerated lowering of the stringent financial standards required of Underwriting Members – first, the acceptance of Sponsored Names with no requirement of a wealth certificate of any kind, followed by the introduction of Mini Names which brought the minimum wealth requirements of a normally qualified Name down from £75,000 to £37,500, and then the relaxation of the wealth certificate requirement itself by allowing a simple 'bank guarantee' rather than the approval by Lloyd's of the assets proffered. Even my own bank, out of the blue, suggested that I used a guarantee from it instead of my wealth certificate for my Lloyd's financial requirements. It was explained that this would not only relieve me of the problem of ensuring that my investments were acceptable to Lloyd's, but I could also use the value of my house which would be acceptable to the bank for them to provide a guarantee to Lloyd's concerning my wealth which, the bank explained, would allow me to increase my premium income limits. In the old days real estate represented by one's main home was not acceptable to Lloyd's as part of a wealth certificate.

Lord Cromer, in his report, said that if Lloyd's was to remain a world player it had to expand its capital base, hence Mini Names, etc. In my opinion, in the then prevailing economic climate the financial standards required by Lloyd's, far from being lowered, should have been substantially increased. Instead of reducing the basic wealth certificate from £75,000 to £37,500, it should have been doubled to £150,000 at least and the permitted premium income should have remained as before. That would have been a more logical way of increasing its capital base. 'Sponsored' Names should have been told to resign.

Many senior members of underwriting syndicates and brokers were becoming more detached from the day-to-day activities within The Room. It was becoming possible, for example, for a person to join the reinsurance treaty department of a broking firm, there learn all the technical intricacies of the treaty reinsurance business, progress to the treaty underwriting office of a managing agency, become the pen underwriter, and be elected to the Committee (or Council) of Lloyd's, with very little personal experience of physically working in The Room itself. To understand the complexities of what went on in The Room one had to have an intimate daily relationship with it, this being the only way in which a real understanding of the world insurance climate was readily obtainable on a day-to-day basis. On one busy occasion I was waiting to see a leading underwriter when a senior director of my company arrived. The underwriter turned to me. 'Graham,' he said, 'is this gentleman your new scratch boy?'

'Yes, sir,' I replied.

Loud guffaws all round!

The appointment of a 'chief executive' from outside the

Lloyd's community was required by the Governor of the Bank of England as part of the price of continued self-regulation. If the enlarged Council or even the previous and smaller Committee was doing its job, it was difficult to see how the appointment of an outsider with the new title of chief executive could properly or possibly fit into the scheme of things, especially such a complex market set-up as Lloyd's which had evolved over hundreds of years. If the existing Council was out of its depth, any outsider would surely simply sink without trace. The very title implies that he would impose his own ideas, thoughts and beliefs, however ill-informed they might be, on all those over whom he had been appointed. That is very unwise in a free market composed of dozens of individual businesses, both large and small, with their own successful or otherwise ideas of good underwriting. It amounted, in my opinion, first to a denial of what Lloyd's was all about, and then a collective abrogation of responsibility. At least the Council of Lloyd's, by itself, consisted of persons who were fully cognisant of what it was all about, either as active underwriters, brokers or Names, and were able to use their respective and collective knowledge usefully in any discussion – particularly if they were, including their chairman, receiving their main remuneration from their normal daily activities.

'Chief executive' is a modern designation which does not mean a thing when applied to numerous firms of varying sizes conducting their businesses under one roof, all technically in competition with each other but also dependent upon each other, mainly with unwritten rules and practices which had developed over the years and were continuing to develop successfully as the situation required. This organisation was unique and could only advise itself from within. A 'chief executive' would have needed a long-time and very close day-to-day association with the community of Lloyd's to have been given such an appointment – which was, after all, what the job of 'chairman of Lloyd's' was all about anyway. It seemed a perfect recipe for arguments between the chief executive and the chairman of Lloyd's when it is remembered that chairmen of Lloyd's arrived in their position after thirty or so years' experience of a constantly changing market. If ever there was a recipe for 'conflict of interests', this was it.

Unfortunately, at such a critical period in the history of Lloyd's no individual with the stature of John Julius Angerstein, Cuthbert Heath, Arthur Lloyd Sturge, Sir Eustace Pulbrook, to name a few, not to mention Edward Lloyd himself, appeared who was ready, willing and able to lead the recovery back out of the mess which Lloyd's was getting itself into – with one possible exception. This was Bob Kiln, a member of the Committee who was a most successful and knowledgeable underwriter of both insurance and reinsurance business, as is borne out by his book specialising on reinsurance. A calm and relaxed person, not given to saying anything without careful thought, he had strong views about the future of Lloyd's. Unfortunately, his words fell on deaf ears so he resigned from the Committee. He was the person who could have been instrumental in setting the right course at that time.

This unsatisfactory state of affairs was one of the reasons which confirmed my decision to resign my membership of Lloyd's.

The rise in the number of Names in the late 1980s to nearly 35,000 coincided with an unprecedented number of 'normal' and most unusual disasters of various kinds throughout the world which could not have been foreseen, and which directly and indirectly caused a catastrophic downturn in underwriting results at Lloyd's, financially ruining many Names. In 1995, on a cruise ship, I came across a gentleman wearing a blazer with a Lloyd's badge on the pocket, about which I naturally commented. His reaction was one of downright fury, so I asked him to tell me about it over a drink. His story was quite simple: three years after his acceptance as a Name he was sent his first underwriting year's results, which consisted of a demand for a great deal of money to meet his losses, since when he had received more bills, bringing his losses to well over £200,000 – and he still had two more years to run of his initial three years' underwriting cycle. His story was typical of hundreds if not thousands of underwriting Names who had been attracted by the magic, charisma, call it what you will, of being a 'member of Lloyd's'. Public figures, politicians, socialites, all stampeded into joining the 'let my money work twice for me' club. In the space of a few years many suddenly faced ruin for doing something which at the time seemed to be 'a jolly good idea'.

Lloyd's survived the financial nonsenses attendant upon the 'South Sea Bubble', but failed to ensure that something not entirely dissimilar would not happen about three hundred years later.

To summarise what I believe went wrong:

1. Reducing the financial requirements;

2. Broking firms being required to divest themselves of their underwriting activities;

3. Permitting foreigners to become Names, thereby opening Lloyd's through its foreign members to possible foreign jurisdictions (here I am *not* referring to the Service of Suit Clause in individual insurance contracts);

4. Breaching the 20 Per Cent Rule concerning foreign financial ownership of interests within the market; this was akin to letting the competition in through the front door where it could then interfere with the natural market forces;

5. Over-enlargement by positive recruitment of Names and general incompetence in the handling of such enlargement;

6. The amount of available insurance expertise failing to keep up with the huge expansion in underwriting capacity consequent upon the introduction of so many new Names. In this context I include successful underwriters in their own class searching for premium income from those classes which they did not understand, for example, LMX;

7. The decision imposed by the government via the Governor of the Bank of England to appoint a chief executive from outside Lloyd's;

8. The excitement about the totally unnecessary new building (the 'oil refinery');

9. Proliferation of dubious offshore activities;

10. The development of inter-relationship of wholly non-Lloyd's interests in joint underwriting situations, particu-

larly in the Third Party Liability or Casualty sector;

11. Underwriting agencies 'going public';

12. More than one member of a family being permitted to become a Name.

Many Names, caught up with the collective results of some Third Party Liability (Casualty) underwriting, were subjected to horrendous losses to such a wide-ranging extent that the Council of Lloyd's put into effect a scheme to mitigate the accumulated financial misery which affected thousands of people. The aim of this resourceful rescue operation was twofold – first, to keep the Lloyd's market as a world leader in the insurance business and, second, to help those Names who faced financial disaster. It is generally known as the Lloyd's Reconstruction and Renewal (R & R) Plan to reinsure liabilities of Lloyd's syndicates for the years of account up to and including 1992. Its purpose is to administer the run-off of these liabilities. As part of this, the Equitas Group was formed to undertake these responsibilities. This wise and profound plan involves the liabilities relating to more than 740 Lloyd's 'syndicate years' including more than 580 'open years'.

It was a bold undertaking involving mathematical calculations concerning losses advised upon which an immediate Reserve sum is set, and until that Reserve is paid such sum will be earning interest (if you have a loss, declare it and earn interest on it until that loss is actually paid). Such a very courageous scheme could only have been devised with the co-operation and assistance of the types of persons who have always been working at Lloyd's. From what I can gather, no longer being an underwriting member myself, it has been received with mixed feelings but, wisely, the vast majority of underwriting members appear to have accepted it. A few, apparently, did not. This scheme, together with 'corporate underwriting members' who now form by far the larger proportion of the overall underwriting capacity, should ensure the continued existence of Lloyd's as a great insurance market which has been forced by circumstances to abandon the principle of membership being contingent upon unlimited personal liability. Lloyd's current (1999) overall premium income stands at around £9 billion.

★

I regard myself as being privileged to have been part of the Lloyd's community and very personally involved in its careful expansion after World War II. I feel extremely sad that a combination of incompetent seniors, both brokers and underwriters, a general lowering of personal standards and attitudes, and ignorant interference by outsiders, including politicians, almost caused its total demise. I do believe that with its new arrangements Lloyd's is firmly set once again on a successful future, will continue to lead the world in the business of innovative insurances, and be ready to fulfil any new insurance need as and when it occurs.

Postscript: Nine Eleven

The worst catastrophe to strike the United States since Pearl Harbor occurred on Tuesday, September 11 2001, when four aircraft on regular domestic flights were hijacked. Two were flown into the Twin Towers of the World Trade Center in New York City. Another crashed into the Pentagon in Washington DC. The journey of the fourth, on its way to a destination undisclosed by the hijackers, was cut short and came down in a field in Pennsylvania through the extraordinary bravery of its passengers and crew who attacked the hijackers. There were no survivors.

Nine Eleven, as it is now known, was also the worst day in the history of my late employers, Marsh & McLennan Companies. The employees who were located on floors 48 through 54 in 2 World Trade Center were safely evacuated, but 295 of their colleagues who occupied floors 93 through 100 in 1 World Trade Center, where the first aircraft hit the building, lost their lives. Staff were relocated to MMC's headquarters at 1166 Avenue of the Americas and other locations. A Family Assistance Centre to provide support and information for families was opened at the Millennium Hotel in midtown Manhattan. An Employees Assistance Centre providing individual and group counselling was set up in 1166 Avenue of the Americas. An MMC Victims Relief Fund was established to support the health, welfare and education needs of the families of employees affected by the tragedy. MMC initiated the fund with a very substantial donation. A memorial service held on 28 September in St Patrick's Cathedral in midtown Manhattan was attended by the mayor of New York, Rudolph Giuliani.

The way this was handled makes me proud to have been a part of the MMC family during my insurance career.

It was a personal shock to watch on television the appalling events of Nine Eleven. I recall during early visits to New York seeing the original buildings in the area being torn down, the ground prepared, and the World Trade Center gradually emerging to add a new concept to the city's skyline.

Many insurance businesses gravitated to the World Trade Center upon the completion of the buildings. On various occasions I spent time in and around the Twin Towers complex and had enjoyable business lunches in the 'Windows on the World' restaurant.

The impact of the disaster on the insurance industry has been heavy and will impinge upon the entire range of insurance from Aviation through Physical Damage, Consequential Loss, Third Party Liabilities, Personal Accident, Life Assurance, and even Marine insurance where vessels had to be diverted to other ports from New York. Claims are to be in excess of $50 billion. Obviously, they might eventually total a great deal more. It will be many months, if not years, before the full insurance and reinsurance implications of Nine Eleven will be finally assessed.

Many very complicated arguments will undoubtedly develop over this disaster and all will depend upon the wordings in the various insurance and reinsurance contracts involved. Will the twin towers be considered as one loss although they were struck minutes apart by two separate aircraft? Will the aircraft which was brought down in a field in Pennsylvania be considered a separate incident? Will the aircraft that crashed into the Pentagon also be looked upon as a separate incident? Or might all four be considered to have been involved in one incident – designated 'Nine Eleven'? Where should the attaching points in the many and various reinsurance contracts occur – and how should they all interlock, if at all? How will War Exclusion clauses be interpreted?

As for Marsh & McLennan, business has righted itself, but the personal loss and grief will take some time to heal.